BAGORE-KI-HAVELI

A Royal Edifice Restored to its Pristine Glory

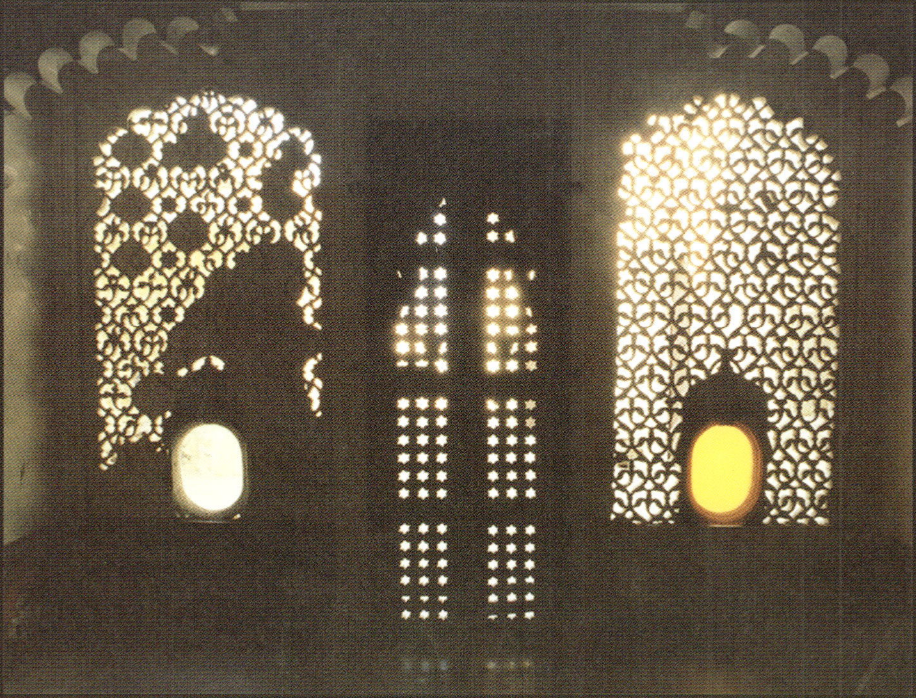

Compiled by
Piers Helsen
with help of Renee Porte

COVER PHOTO BY
KAMLESH DWIVEDI
PHOTO SPECTRUM
BARODA

PHOTOGRAPHY BY
REX STUDIO & KALARTHI STUDIO
UDAIPUR

Designed by
Creative Connection, Udaipur

Published & printed by
D.K. Printworld (P) Ltd.
'Sri Kunj', F-52, Bali Nagar, New Delhi - 110 015 Tel: 545 3975, 546 6019 Fax: +91-11-546 5926 email: dkprintworld@vsnl.net
West Zone Cultural Centre
Bagore-Ki-Haveli, Gangaur Ghat, Udaipur, Rajasthan, India
Tel: +91 294 422567, 410539 Fax : 523858 email : wzcccom_jplsancharnet.in / wzcccom@rediffmail.com Website : www.indiaculture.org

ISBN: 81-246-0206-9

Rs. 95

THE HISTORY OF BAGORE -KI- HAVELI

Bagore-ki-Haveli was built by Shri Amarchand Badwa, the Prime Minister of Mewar between 1751 and 1778, during the reigns of Maharanas Pratap Singh II, Raj Singh II, Ari Singh and Hamir Singh. It isn't certain how long Badwa lived there, but it is recorded that he was poisoned to death. After his death, the haveli came under the domain of Mewar state and was given to the Maharaj of Bagore, a close relative of the Maharana.

The significance of Bagore can be traced back to the mid-seventeenth century. The noblemen and ministers of Mewar were each granted a territory *(thikana)* for the services rendered to the state or as a special mark of favour by the Maharana. There were sixteen *thikanas* spread out around Mewar. Among these were Bansi, Bohera, Karjali, Devgarh, Bagore, Shivrati, Kanod, Salumbar, Sadri and Gogunda. Bagore is actually a village in the Bhilwara district of Mewar. Maharaj Nath Singhji had been the first to ascend to the throne of the Bagore *Jageer*. He was the second son of Maharana Sangram Singh II (1710 1734).

Photos on previous pages:

Front Cover
The Upper Gallery, Tulsi Chowk.

Inside Cover
(Clockwise from top left)
Rang Kaksh(The Kama Sutra Room).
Shringar Kaksh(Princess' Dressing Room) .
Shayan Kaksh(Bedroom).
Baithak (Sitting Room).

Title Page
Intricate pierced screen in an anteroom off Tulsi Chowk.

The *haveli* was suitable to accommodate the large, extended family of the Maharaj of Bagore. In 1838, the Maharana of Mewar, Jawan Singh died childless, so an heir was adopted from the Bagore family. Over the years, various other Maharanas of Mewar died without issue. Maharanas Sardar Singh, Swaroop Singh, Shambhu Singh and Sajjan Singh were all adopted from Bagore family, having spent their childhood and youth playing in its *chowks*.

There were distinct areas within the *haveli* for the different members of the family. The *durrie khana* and the mirrored passage *(kanch mahal)* were within the men's area. The *maharaj* and his guests used this area for living, sleeping and working.

Maharaj Shakti Singh was responsible for the construction of the beautiful *Kanch Mahal* over the triple arched gate in 1878. However Shakti Singh brought disfavour on himself by plotting against his nephew, Maharana Sajjan Singh, and was exiled from the State. Shakti Singh left no male heir, and after his death, Thikana of Bagore was dissolved. The *haveli* was confiscated (declared *khalsa)* during the reign of the next maharana, Fateh Singh (1884-1930). His successor, Maharana Bhupal Singh (1930-1955) renovated the *haveli* into a grade III guesthouse, where palace guests could be accommodated, and in fact there used to be a tunnel system that lead directly to the City Palace.
After the *haveli* was handed over to the WZCC, an attempt was made to reopen this tunnel, which had been out of use for several years. The attempt had to be abandoned when it was found that the foundations of two new buildings in the Lalghat area were blocking the former passageway completely.

Gangaur Ghat & Bagore-ki-Haveli

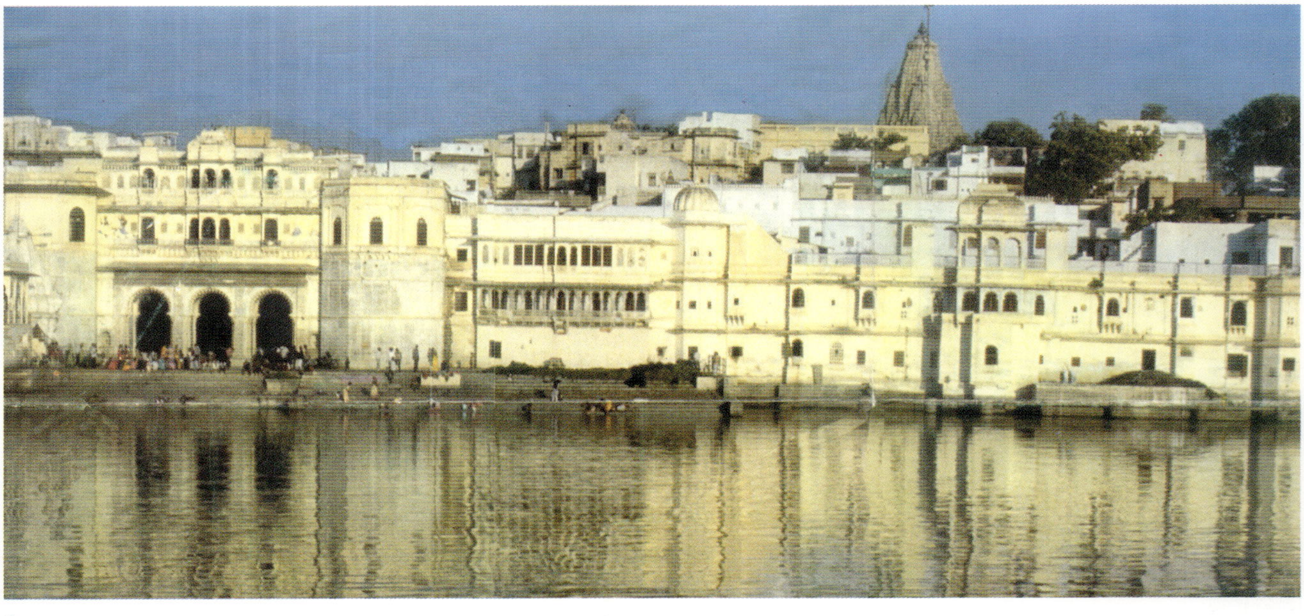

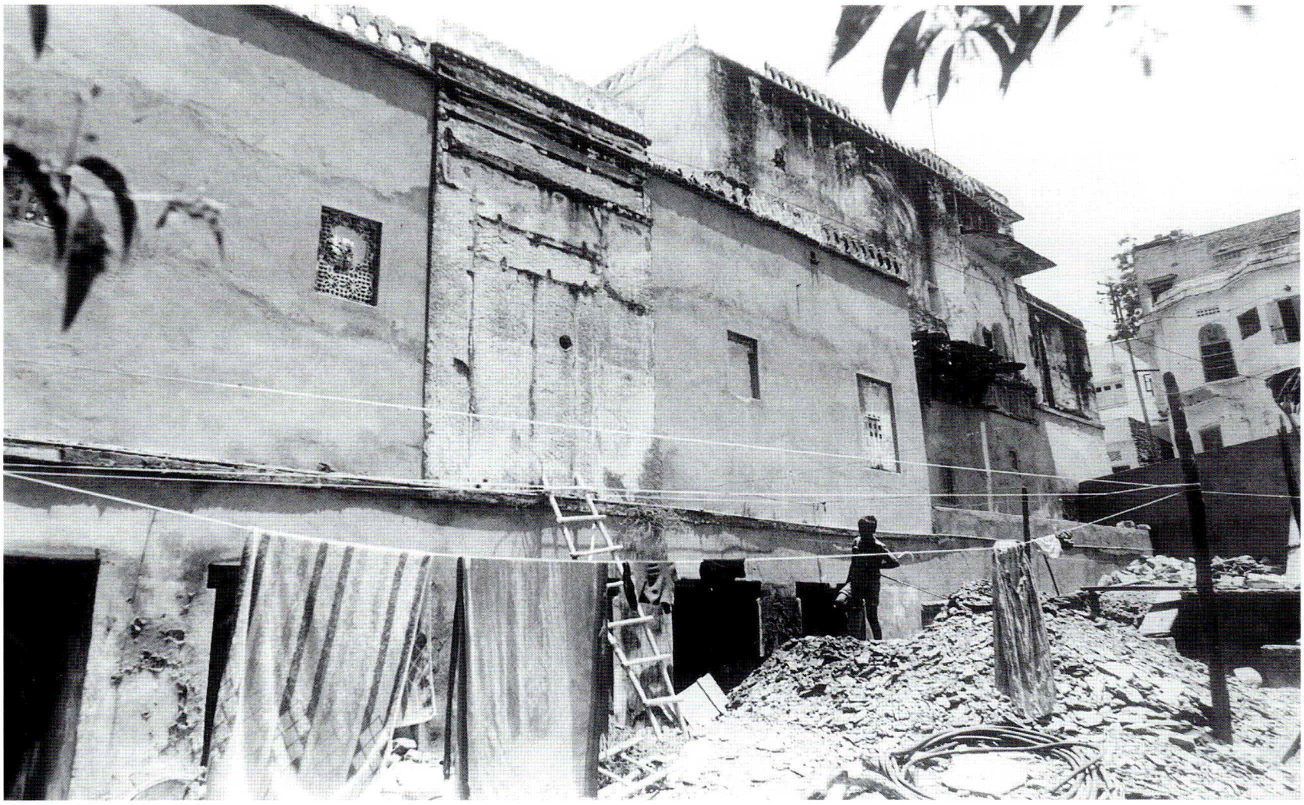

RESTORATION

A testimony to the years of neglect that brought the haveli to the nadir of its existence. Vandalism, inappropriate structural modifications, lack of interest, theft of materials, erosion and invasive vermin all took their toll.

Following the integration of Mewar State into Rajasthan in 1947, the *haveli* came under the control of the Public Works Department of the Government of Rajasthan, who utilized it for the housing of government employees. It suffered a lengthy period of neglect, with people encroaching upon the rooms and adding alien building elements.
The frequent change in usage led to many alterations and additions, ruining the character of the *haveli,* and gradually it lost its architectural splendour and elegant proportions.
In 1986, it was handed over to the West Zone Cultural Centre for housing its headquarters.

The West Zone Cultural Centre thought it appropriate to convert the *haveli* into a museum because of its charming style, typical of the very best Mewari architecture, though with a unique character of its own.

The plan was that it should be restored as faithfully as possible as an example of how a *haveli* would have looked and how life there would have been.

After five years of strenuous restoration work, and the investment of a huge amount of money, a beautifully restored Bagore-ki-Haveli now depicts the royal lifestyle, architecture and cultural ethos in its pristine glory.

The working team included local masons and artisans; some of whom had received training at the 'Institute for Revival of Traditional Building Arts' at Amber, near Jaipur. Experts and members of the nobility were consulted to give each room an accurate glimpse of the royal past.

Several 18th & 19th century frescoes were uncovered beneath many layers of whitewash during restoration. The doors, windows and perforated screens were repaired and restored to their original form.

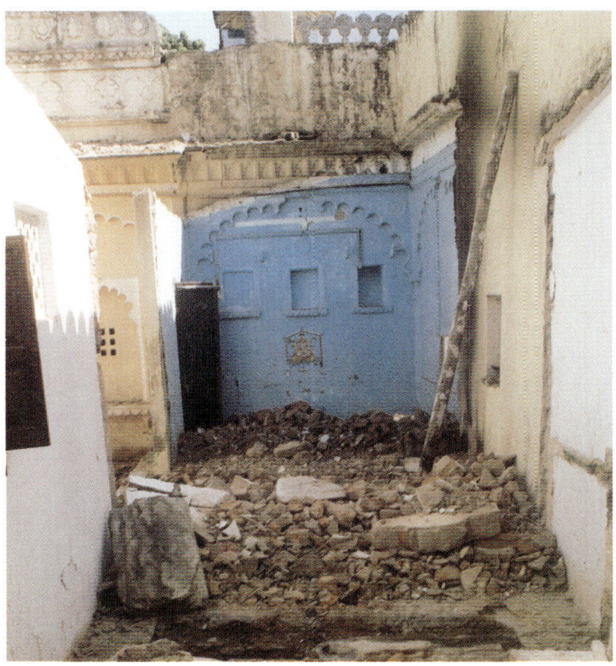

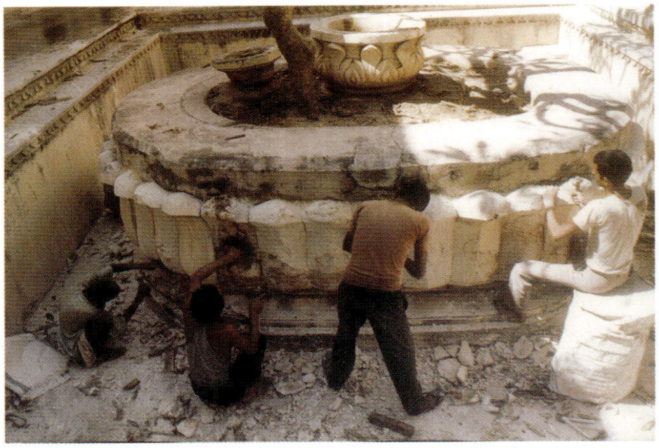

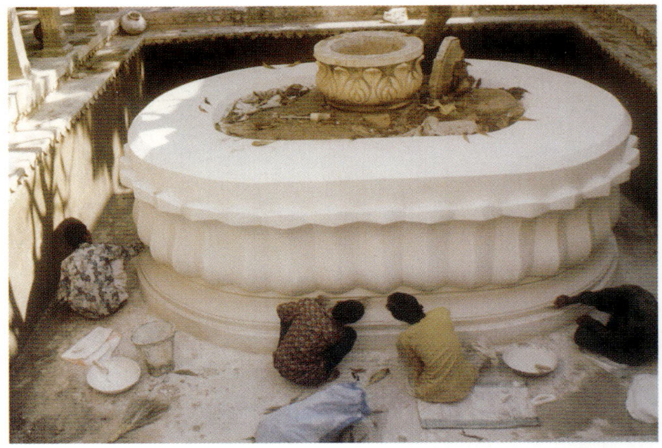

During and after views of the exacting renovation work on the Lotus Pool, Kamal Chowk.

(Below) Detail of stone carving that is finished with a coating of aaraish (lime plaster).

(Bottom) A craftsman carefully restoring an ancient fresco.

AARAISH WORK (LIME PLASTERING)

Even though stone was, by and large, used in construction work in Udaipur, the inner walls of the living quarters of the *havelis* were covered with a very smooth plaster coating that had a marble finish. The technique is known as *aaraish, ghutai* or *sandala.* The process of preparing this lime plaster is elaborate and troublesome.

For some of the external surfaces on the facade of the *haveli,* coloured finishes had been used in the past, using stone pigments in the plaster mix to obtain the required yellow or grey finish. These stone pigments were derived from pure crushed stone of that colour and do not fade in sunlight.

A highly skilled craftsman was able to complete only one square foot of *aaraish* work after working laboriously for the entire day, since the work had to be carried out over sculptured stone columns, brackets and *jharokhas.* Seven to eight skilled masons were deployed to carry out the *aaraish* work for the *haveli.* Each of the masons had about seven apprentices.

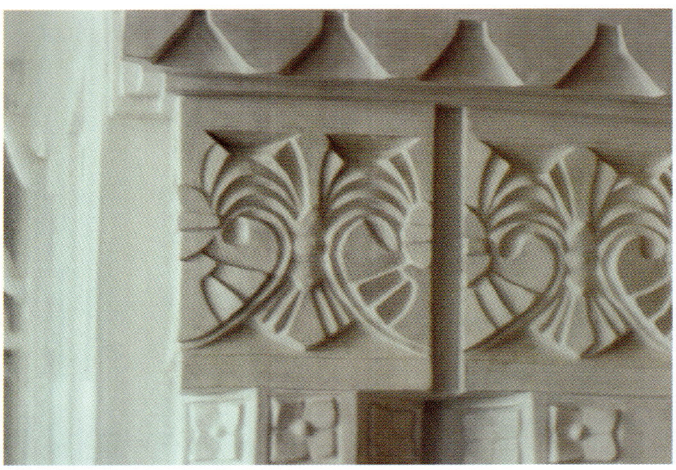

GLASSWORK

During the era of *haveli*-building in Udaipur, the maharana of the time owned a glass factory in Belgium, and it supplied all the coloured glass used in the *jali* work.

The City Palace as well as all the *havelis* in Udaipur were enriched with this ready supply of beautiful glass, but the factory eventually closed down and the supply of coloured glass from that source stopped.

For the restoration work at Bagore-ki-Haveli, original Belgian coloured glass was obtained from junk vendors *(kabadiwalas)* or from other *havelis,* which were either being demolished or were in a severe damaged condition.

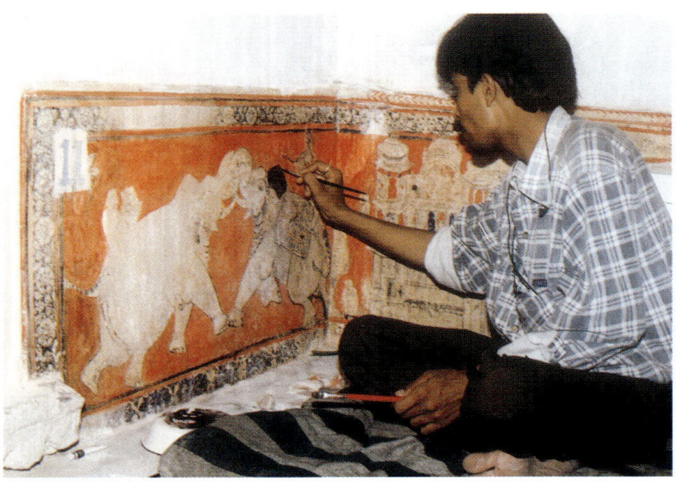

FRESCOES

It was found that many of the frescoes had been damaged, especially those in the *Rang Mahal.* These had to be restored. The work of renovating the frescoes was carried out by a team of skilled craftsmen from the National Museum in Delhi.

Fresco painting is carried out using the powders of various stones mixed with gum. The juices and extracts from various trees and specific leaves are used in the mix. The paint is then applied to fresh *aaraish* work.

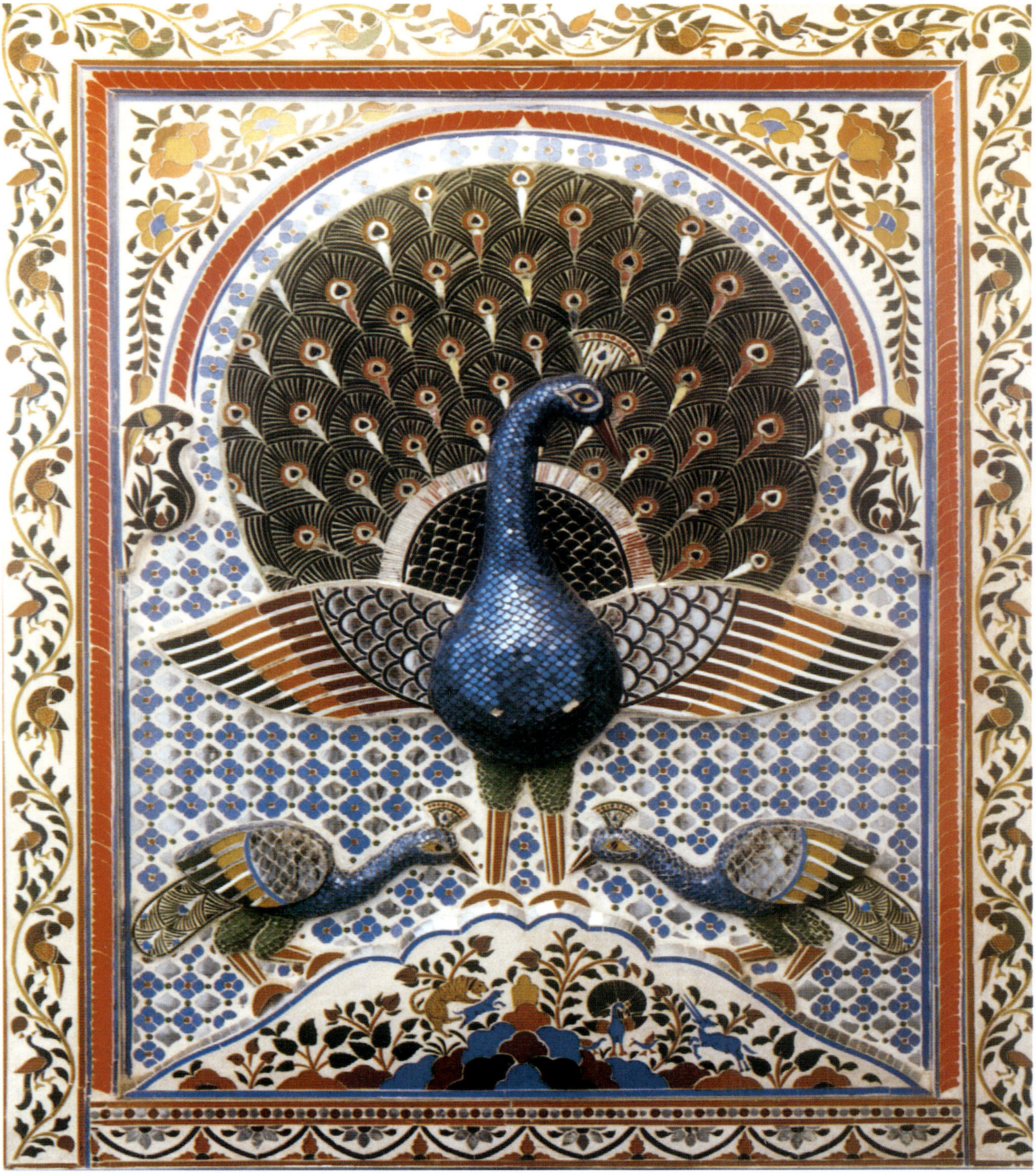

MIRROR INLAY WORK

Examples of this work are to be found in the *Rang Mahal*, in the *Badi Burz* and in the *Mor Durrie Khana*. The mirrors are placed on a base of lime plaster. A special finish is then applied, produced from a paste of baked lime, crushed brick and water. The surface is now ready to receive the relief work. The general design is carved out, which is followed by the finer details worked out in a paste. Finally, the mirrors are cut into the desired shape and their edges softened. The pieces are then painstakingly placed to form the desired pattern.

THE PEACOCK

A magnificent panel of traditional mirror work situated on the first floor gallery of Tulsi Chowk.

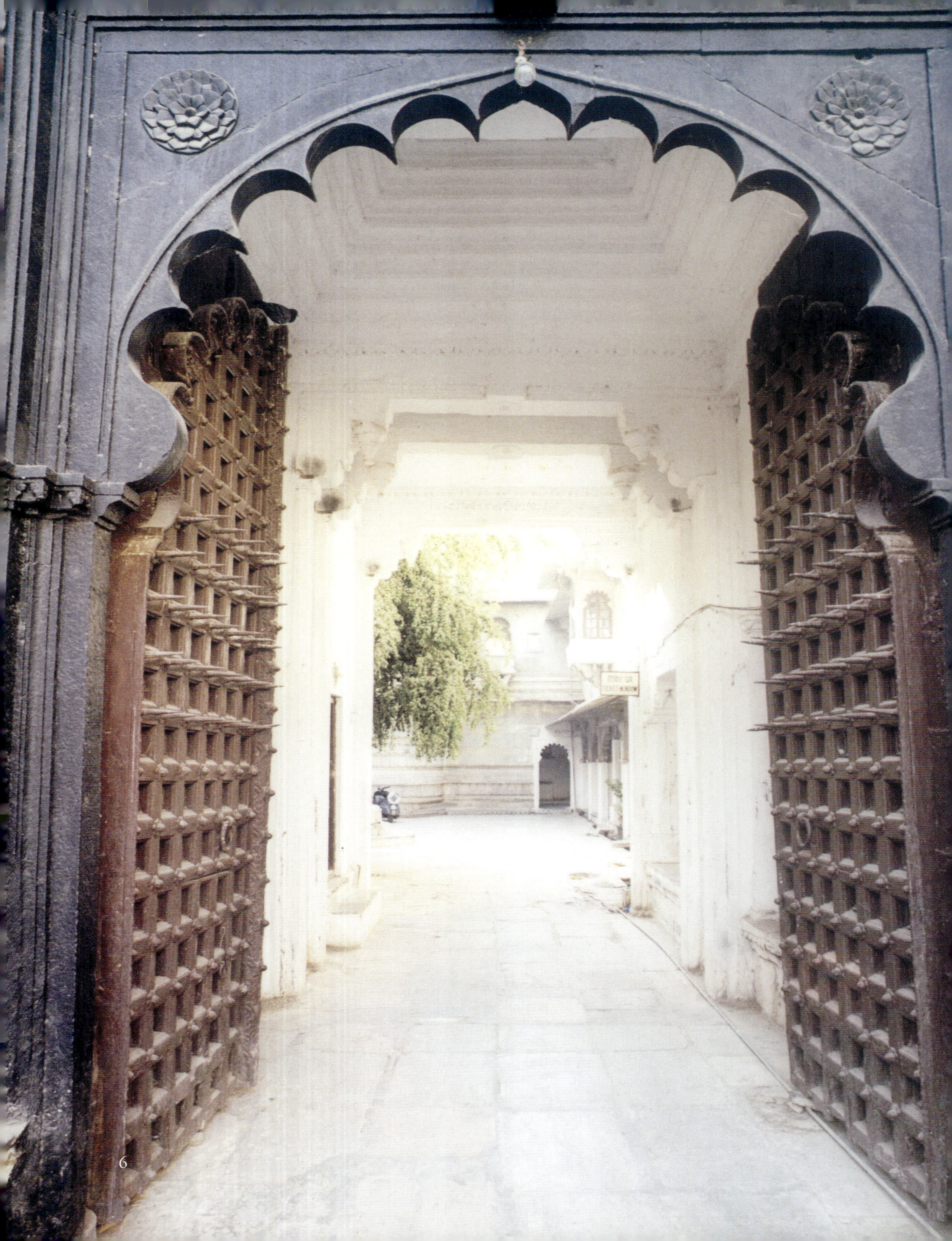

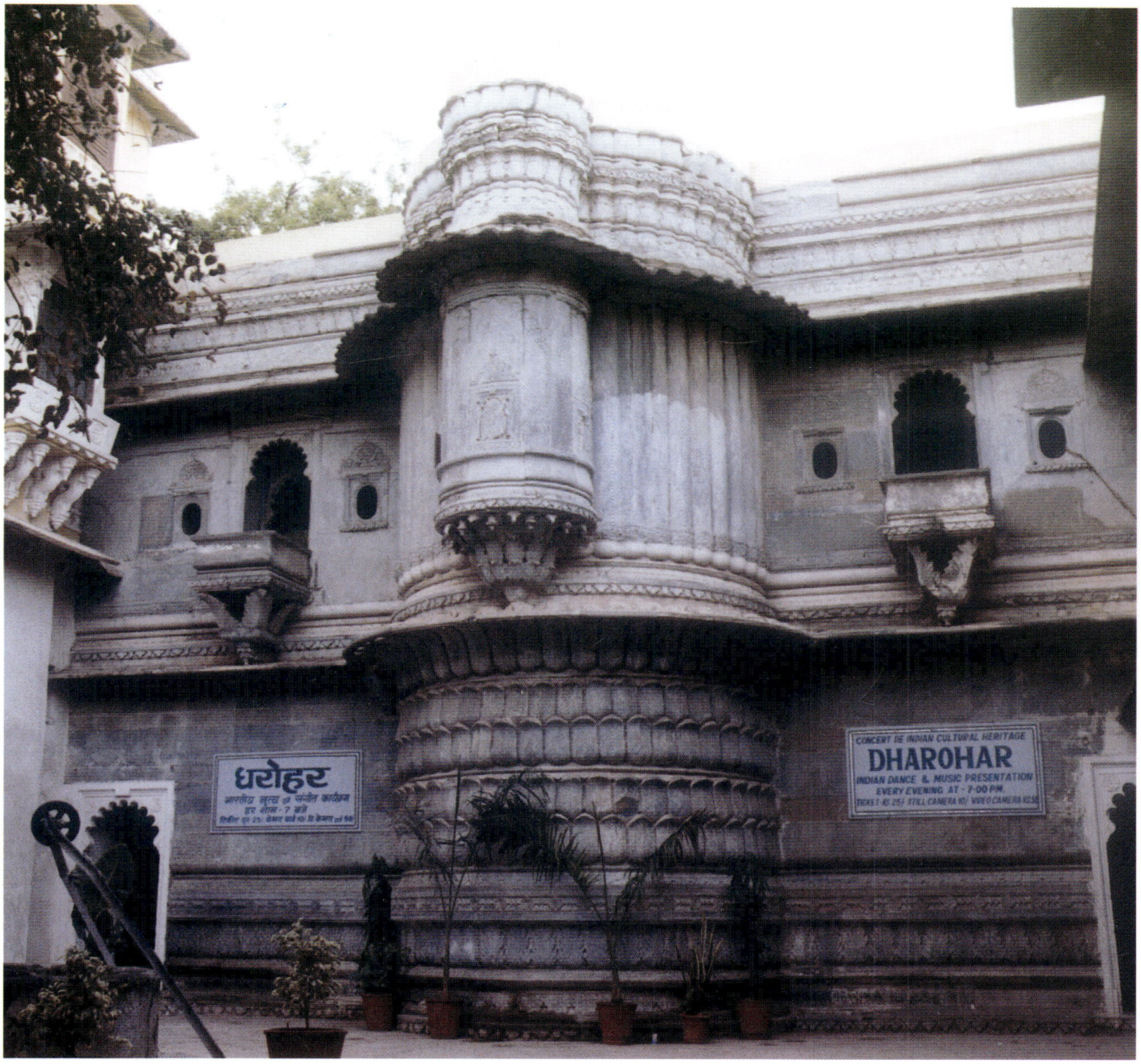

KUAN CHOWK

THE LOTUS FOUNTAIN

This unique structure once functioned as a fountain; the water spewing from narrow pipes set above the overhanging 'petals' at the first floor level. The well can be seen in the foreground to the left.

BAGORE-KI-HAVELI

Bagore-ki-Haveli is situated on the banks of Lake Pichola. It has 138 rooms several balconies, terraces and courtyards and is notable for its typical Mewari architecture, exquisite glass inlay work and paintings. The *haveli* is situated at Gangaur Ghat by the side of Lake Pichola barely 100 metres from the City Palace and Jagdish Temple. The *haveli* overlooks Jag Niwas (which is now the renowned Lake Palace Hotel) and Jag Mandir, where the Mughal Prince Khurram took refuge, who was to later become Emperor Shahjehan- the creator of Taj Mahal.

KUAN CHOWK (WELL COURT)

On passing through the impressive main gates of Bagore-ki-Haveli, one enters an attractive, leafy courtyard, the centre of which is occupied by a well. On the southern side of this courtyard, is the Lotus Fountain, a fascinating two-storied fountain from whence water cascaded, cooling and refreshing the air. It is the most attractive and unusual structure of sandstone, decorated with profuse carving. As yet, it has not been restored to working order. The activities of the household staff were performed around the ground floor of *Kuan Chowk*, and the stores, the oil mills and the stables were located here. The servants lived in separate quarters across Lake Pichola.

Photo on previous page:

The Great entrance to Bagore-ki-Haveli.

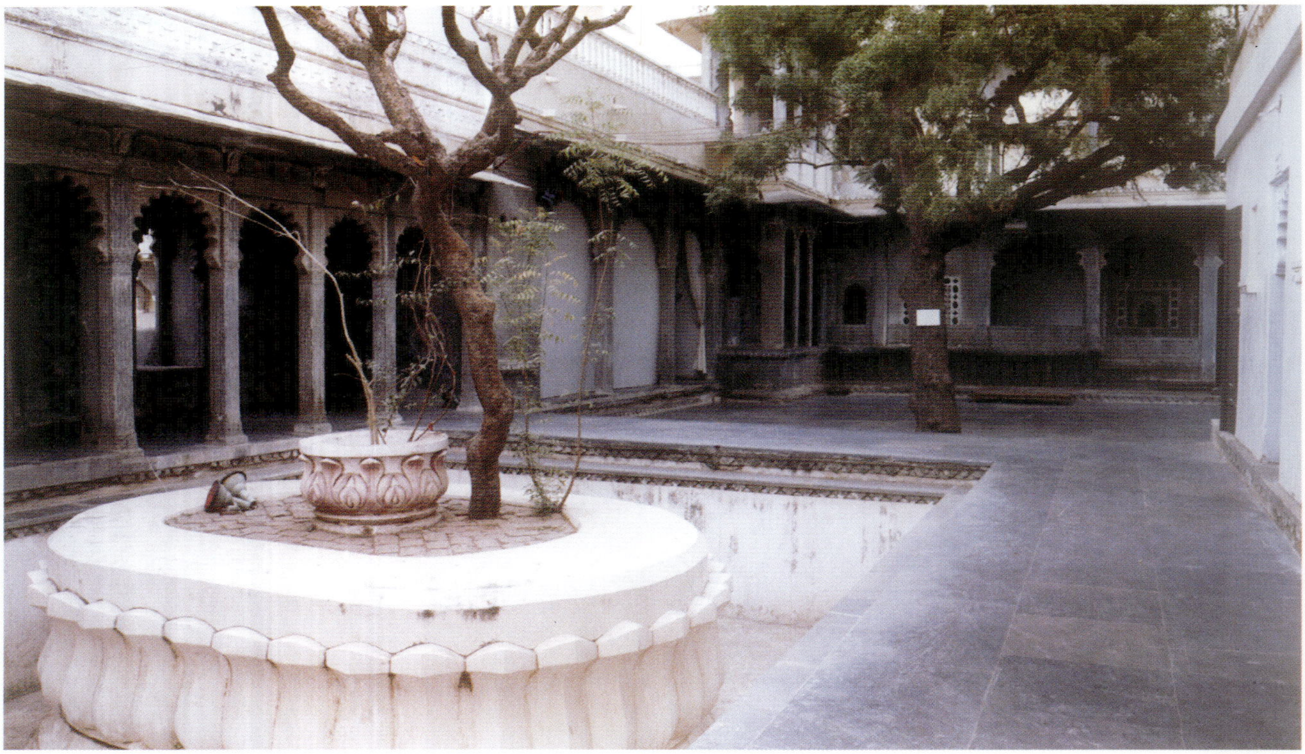

The now empty Lotus Pond in Kamal Chowk. Neem Chowk can be seen in the background.

THE ZENANA

Strict rules regarding segregation of the sexes were rigidly observed in Rajasthan until fairly recently, and this was even more particularly maintained amongst the higher caste families. Even today, some Rajasthani communities, more usually those residing in rural areas, continue this practice. The royal ladies were kept in *purdah* (a curtain). The women's quarters, known as the *zenana,* tended to occupy more space than the men's, possibly because there would be a large female contingent; wife, mistresses and maids. In addition, women were confined to the *haveli,* and would therefore required more space for their rather limited world, whereas the men were often away from home, in battle, partying or hunting .

Women performing Ghoomar dance every evening in 'Dharohar' in Neem Chowk.

NEEM CHOWK AND KAMAL CHOWK (LOTUS COURT)

This courtyard, situated on the first floor of the *haveli,* has a *Shiva* temple set against the north wall, enclosed by a pair of magnificent brass covered doors. The ceiling of the temple's portico bears some fine religious paintings, depicting the four *dhams*- the holiest Hindu places of pilgrimage in India. They are the temples in Dwarka Dham, Rameshwaram, Badrinath and Jagannath Puri. The adjoining *Neem Chowk* (*Neem* is a tree that has many beneficial properties) was used for dance and music performances.

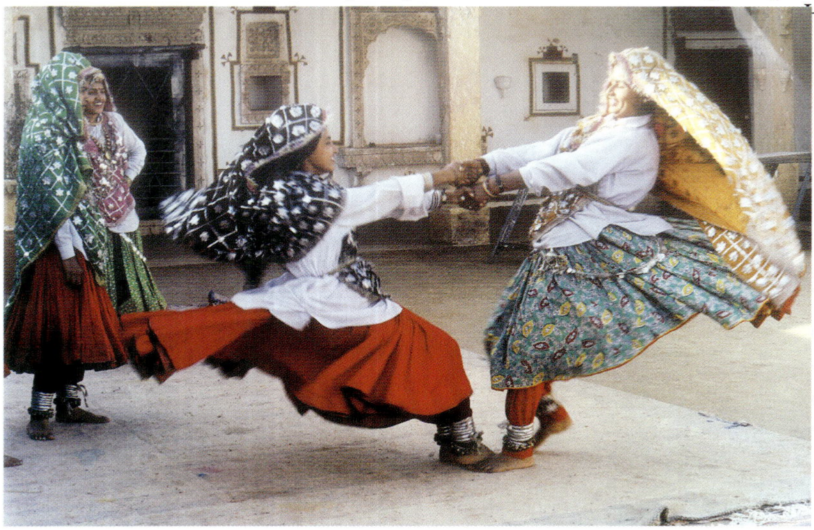

With a degree of continuity in mind, this court now serves as an arena for a variety of authentic performing art forms for the benefit of the public. There are regular evening shows-*'Dharohar',* comprising of dance, mime, music, puppetry, light & shadow shows etc., set in the twin courtyards of *Neem Chowk* and *Kamal Chowk* providing an atmospheric setting with their trees and fine architecture.

TULSI CHOWK

This was the hub of the aristocratic lifestyle of the princesses. The rooms surrounding the *Tulsi Chowk* (meaning Oregano Court) once upon a time housed the women's quarters *(zenana).* This area was strictly off-limits to men, and it would have been a serious breach of protocol for any outside male to enter.

This area has been recreated in minute detail. A hand-operated panel fan in the ceiling, mirrors with carved wooden fixtures on the walls, rooms and balconies decked with traditional cabinets, swings, floor and ceiling coverings are all in their appropriate places. The museum thus displays the private chambers of the ladies, their dressing rooms, bathrooms, living rooms, sleeping quarters, worship room and recreation rooms. The ladies would sometimes use the *Tulsi Chowk* itself to perform the *Ghoomar* & other dances, especially to celebrate fairs and festivals.

Today, in the chambers surrounding the ground floor of this court, there are displays of turbans and women's costumes, and a permanent exhibition devoted to the process of restoration. On the first floor, there is also one room that has been left in an unrestored state, so as to give one an impression of the pre-restoration conditions. Several photographs showing pre & post restoration provide an interesting glimpse of the work carried out.

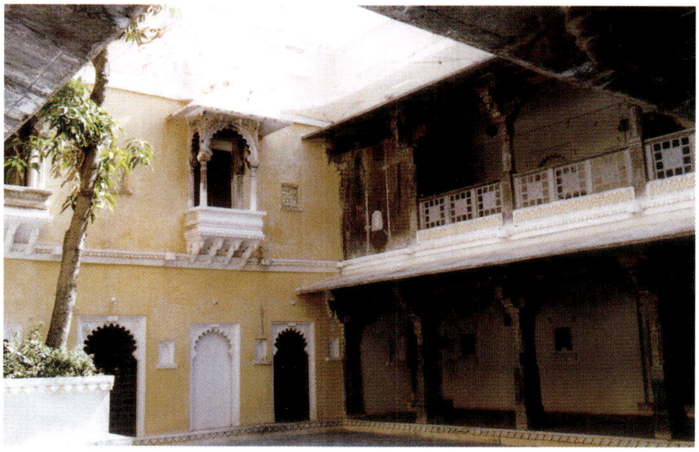

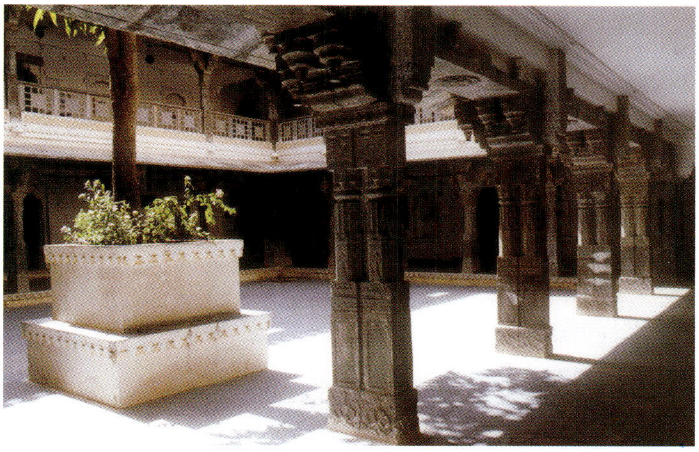

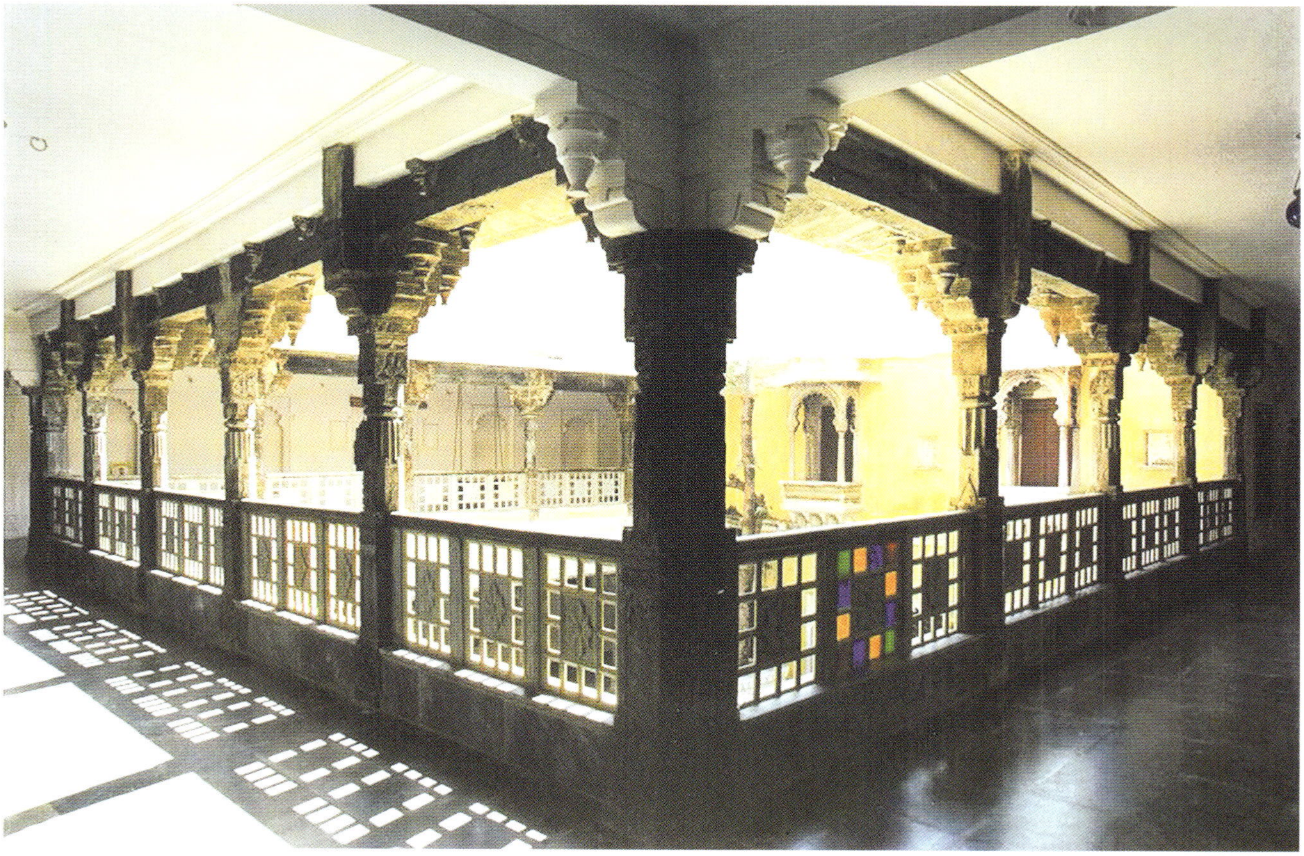

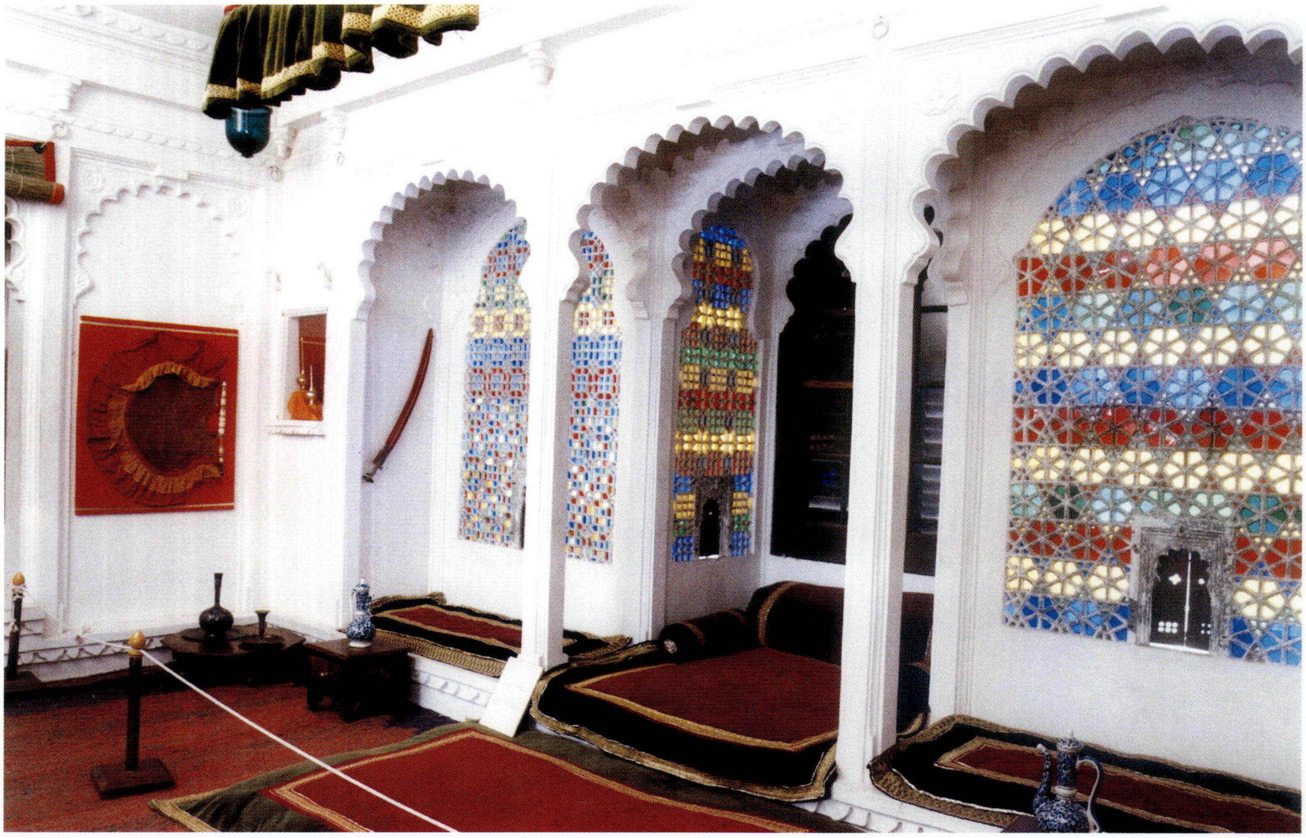

Light, in rainbow colours enriches the luxurious ladies' sitting room.

The bathroom, displaying some of the items of everyday use.

The chambers of the *zenana*, leading off the gallery that surrounds the first floor of *Tulsi Chowk*, have been recreated in the style of the *haveli's* heydays. The furniture, soft furnishings and everyday articles of the royal household are on display.

BAITHAK (SITTING ROOM)

A room where the princesses would relax with their female friends and relatives to discuss issues pertaining to politics, social life or just to chit-chat. This place was called the princesses' *durrie khana.*

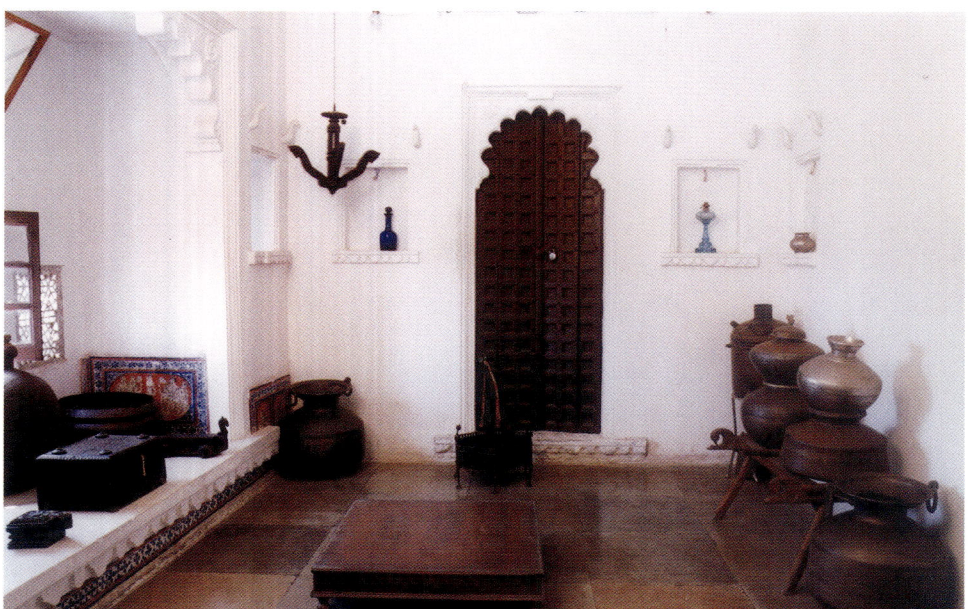

SNANAGAR (BATHROOM)

The ladies' bathroom was supplied with a hip bath *(kundi)* and pitchers *(gola)* made of brass, copper and various metal alloys. The princess would be seated on a wooden platform, with her maids smearing her entire body with a special preparation created from turmeric, gram flour and fresh cream *(pithi)*. Following this, they would rinse her with a fragrant mixture of milk, sandalwood and water.

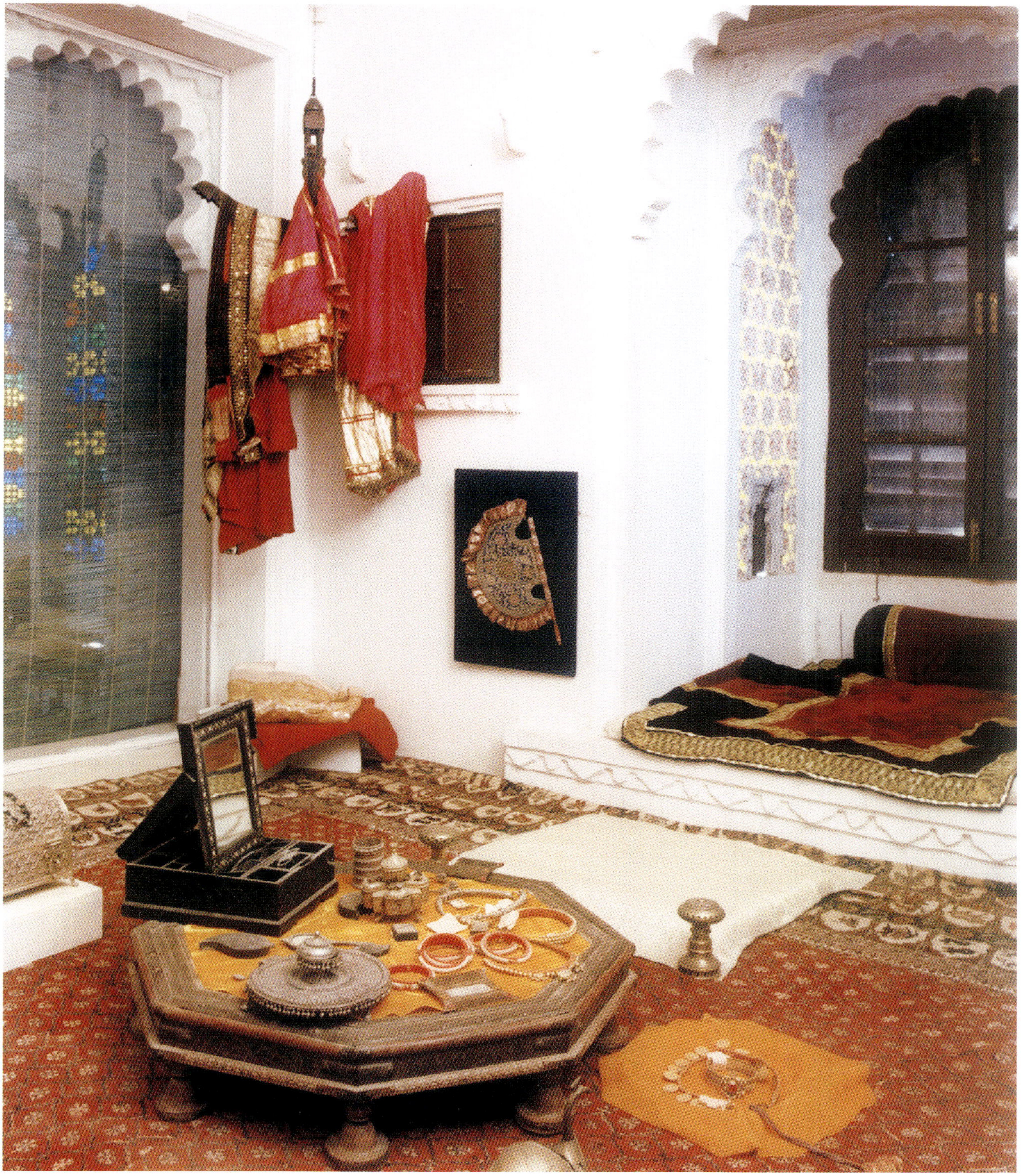

The beautifully endowed Dressing Room.

SHRINGAR KAKSH (DRESSING ROOM)

The dressing room contained wooden trunks, to hold the finery of the princesses. The clothes of the ladies of Mewar varied in colour and style according to the season or the occasion. They wore *falguniya* in February - March *(Falgun)* and *lahariya* in the July - August *(Savan)* period. Also in the room, would be the jewellery boxes and various metal caskets containing valuable ornaments. After dressing, the ladies would apply perfume from the dispenser *(itra-daan)* exhibited in the room. Scent was created from the extracts of roses, jasmine, sandalwood etc.

Photo on the next page: The Entertainment Room

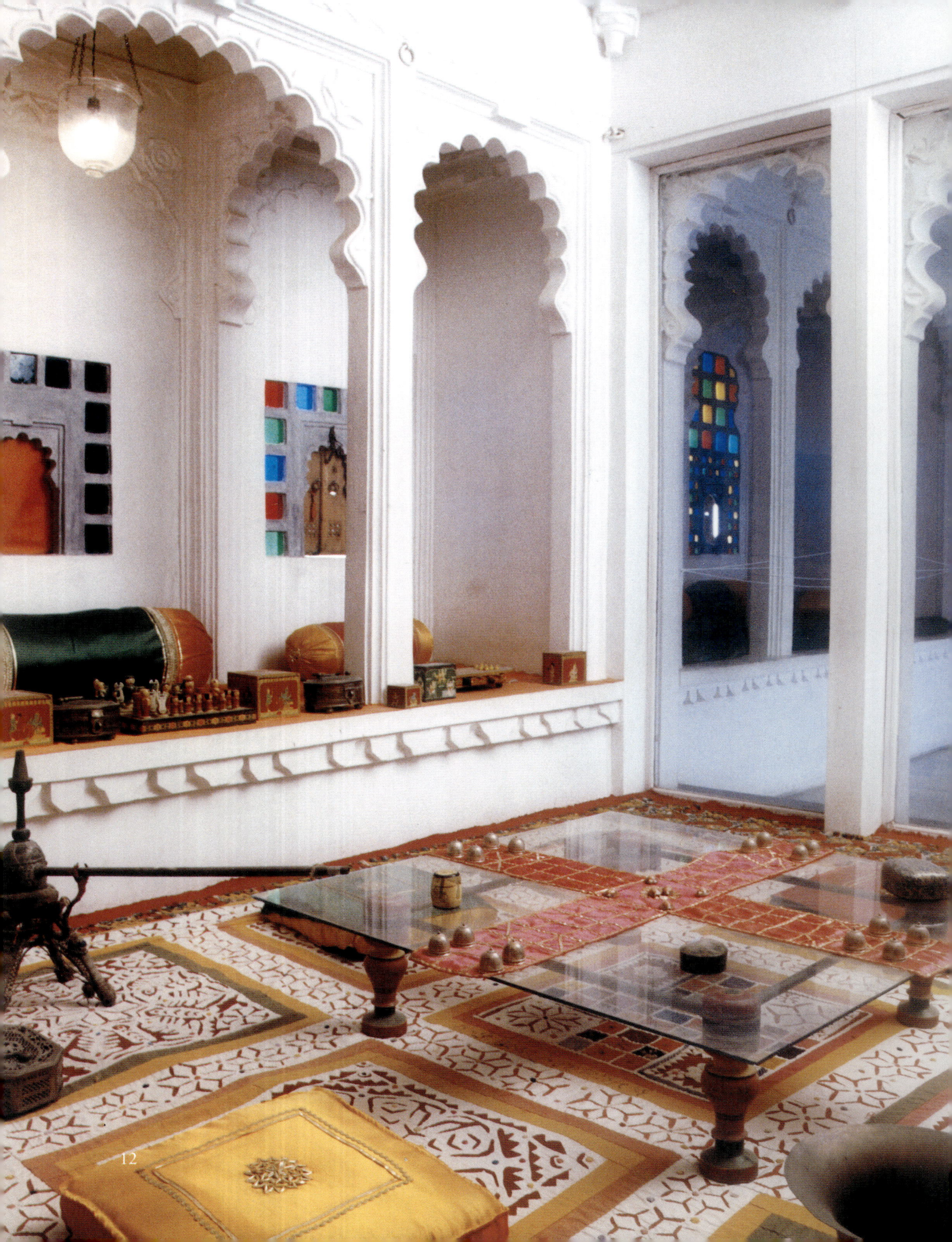

MANORANJAN KAKSH (ENTERTAINMENT ROOM)

Entertainment plays an important role in human life. The royalty and nobility of Mewar enjoyed various board games as means of indoor entertainment. Bagore-ki-Haveli's games room exhibits the popular games of chess, *chaupad*, snakes & ladders and *ganjifa*. The princesses played here during their long hours of confined leisure.

MAJISA-KA-KAMARA (THE MATRIARCH'S CHAMBER)

The quarters of the widowed matriarch has a uniformly white decor; white being a symbol of purity. The rather austere room contained her personal shrine, the portrait of her husband and paintings depicting episodes from the Vedic scriptures etc.

POOJA KAKSH (ROOM OF WORSHIP)

The princesses worshiped their favourite deities within the confines of the *zenana*. A room devoted for this purpose.

GANGAUR KAKSH (THE GANGAUR ROOM)

This small room contains the brightly coloured effigies of *'Gan'* (Lord *Shiva*) and *'Gaur'* (his wife *Parvati*). In Mewar, the *Gangaur* Festival, dedicated to *Gan* and *Gaur*, is celebrated with a grand ceremony. In addition to these two idols, there are a few unrelated objects; a number of toys, wooden horses, dolls and a *chaupad* game.

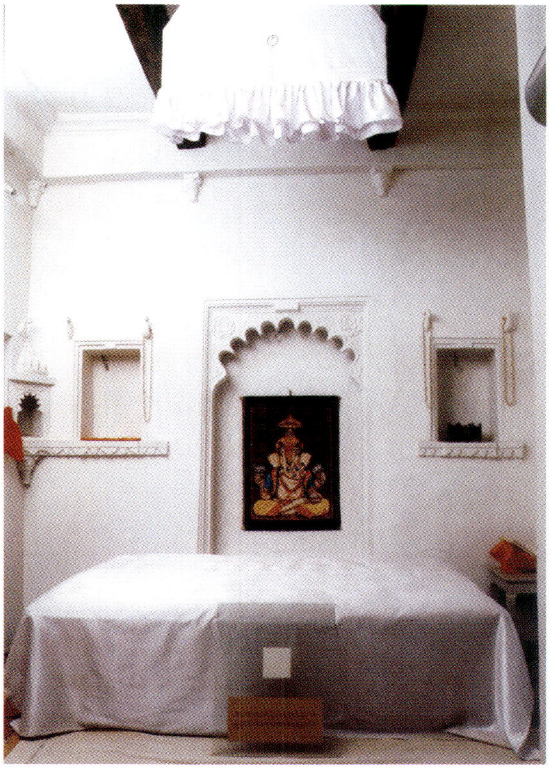

The Matriarch's Chamber & The Room of Worship

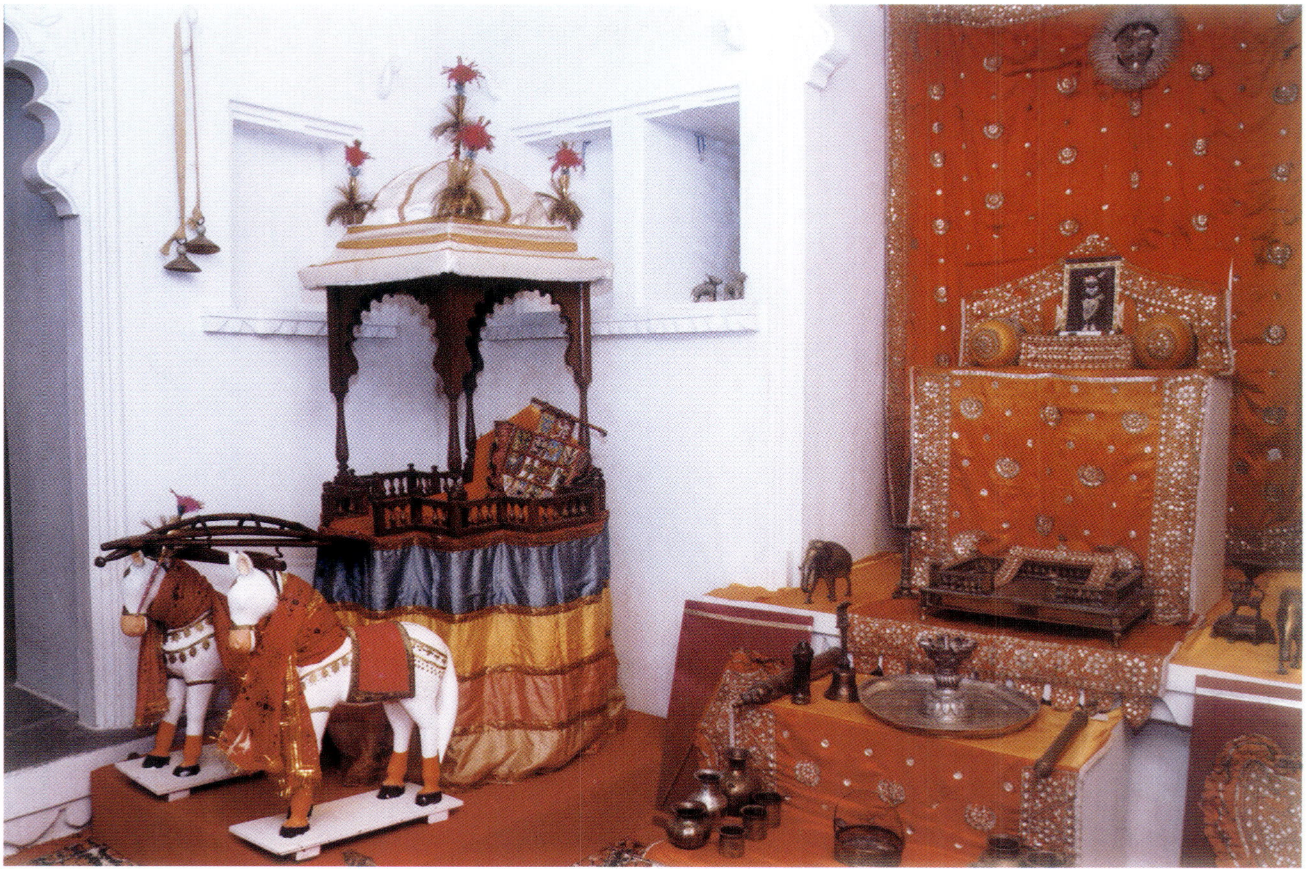

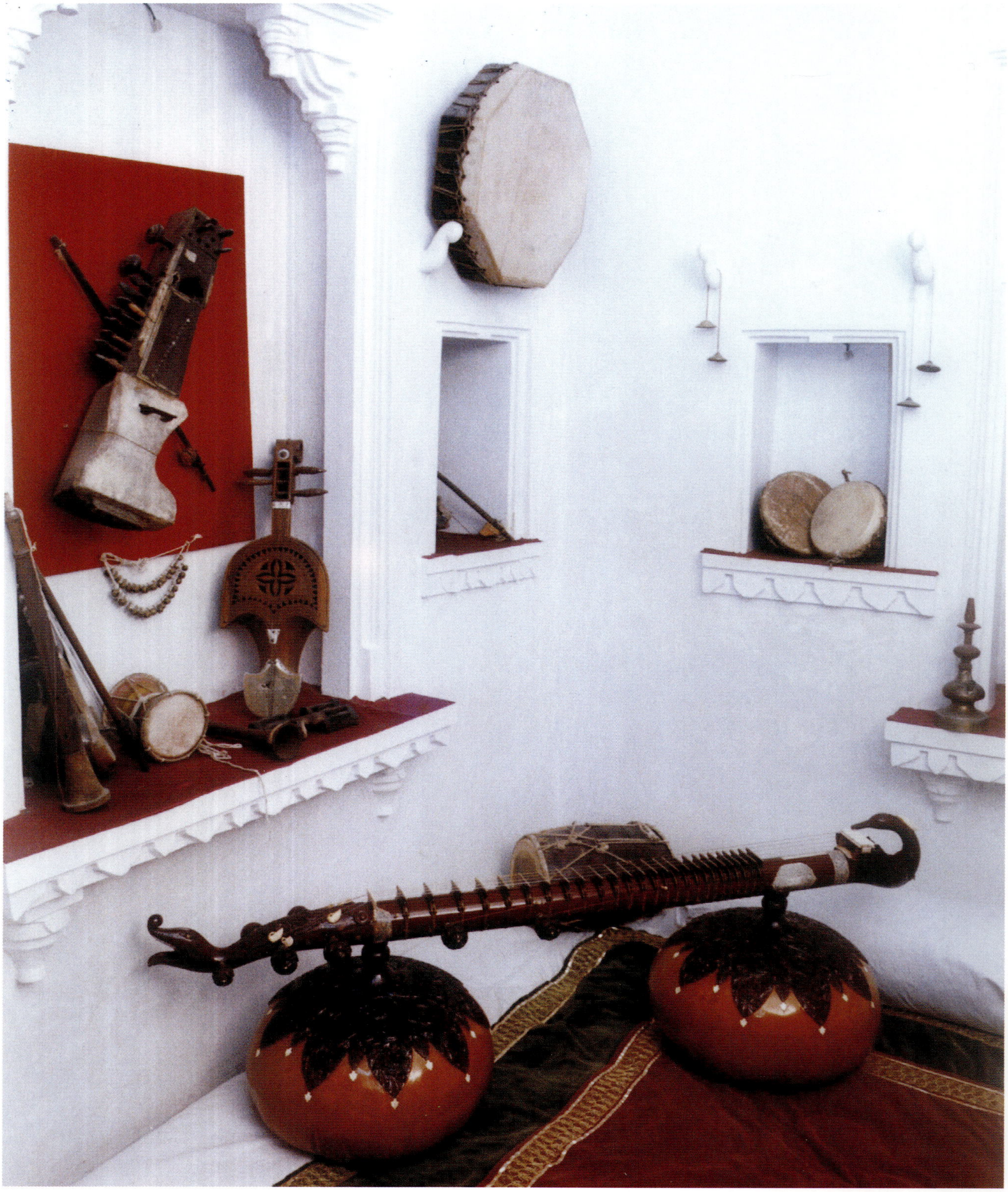

All set for a musical evening in The Music and Study Room.

SANGEET KAKSH (MUSIC ROOM)

Members of the royalty & nobility were great patrons of the arts. Every *haveli* had a music and study room that indicated the inclinations of the occupants towards music and literature. This room was an institution in itself where the ladies learnt music, studied literature and scriptures and would be familiarised with musical instruments such as the *sarangi, nagada, shehnai, dholak*, *santoor, chang,* flute etc.

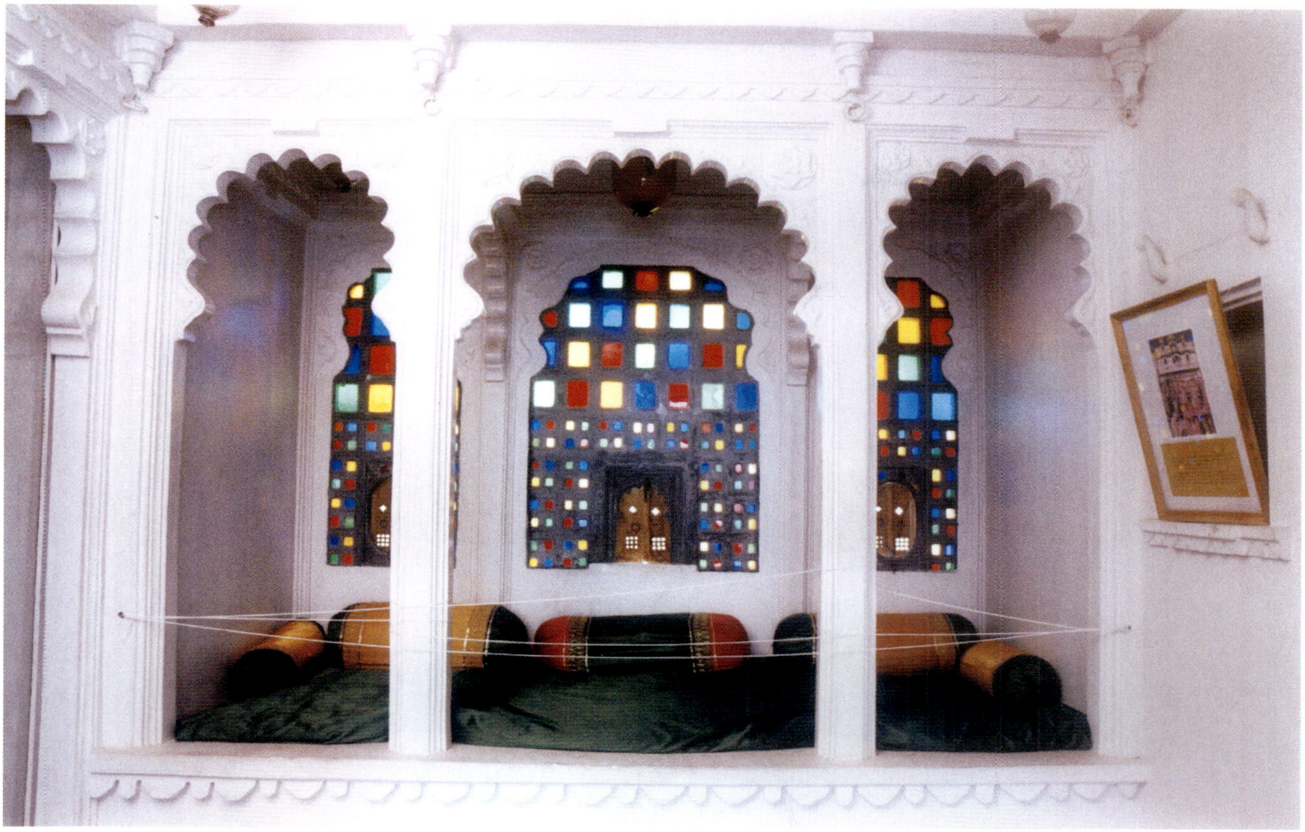

JHAROKHA (BALCONY)

A *jharokha* is a raised balcony platform built into a bay, and is a common feature of *haveli* architecture. The *jharokha* provided a comfortable place to relax, read or chat or to peep through the tiny windows of the bay, so as to observe what was going on below without the risk of being seen.

A jharokha in Bagore-ki-Haveli.

The kitchen, displaying a selection of typical utensils.

SHAYAN KAKSH (BEDROOM)

Bedrooms were arranged in such a fashion that the ladies could be comfortable in all seasons. During the summer, maids *(dawadi)* operated the cloth ceiling fans to ensure the comfort of their mistresses. In winters the rooms were heated using metal hearths *(sigdies)*. The decor of the individual room was according to the taste of the princess. The room had a bed *(dholia)* with mattress, quilt, pillows, hand fans etc. It also had a drinking water arrangement, wooden trunks for clothes and footwear etc.

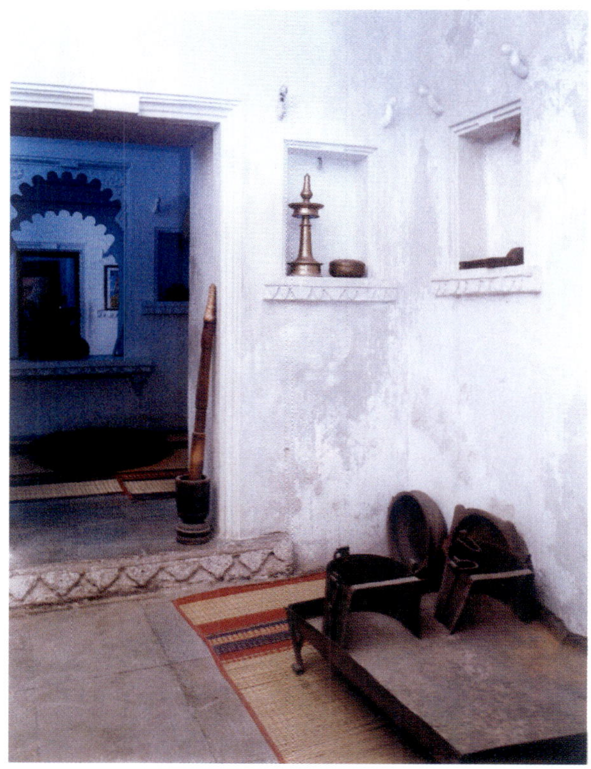

RASODA (KITCHEN)

The *haveli* had a kitchen, equipped with large metal vessels and wooden utensils. Separate pantries existed to store food grains and other provisions.

PARENDA (PLACE FOR DRINKING WATER)

In the *havelis*, drinking water was kept in a place known as the *parenda*, usually situated near the kitchen. In this area, was a terra cotta water storage containers and copper pitchers. From here, water was taken to the apartments of the princesses in small pitchers.

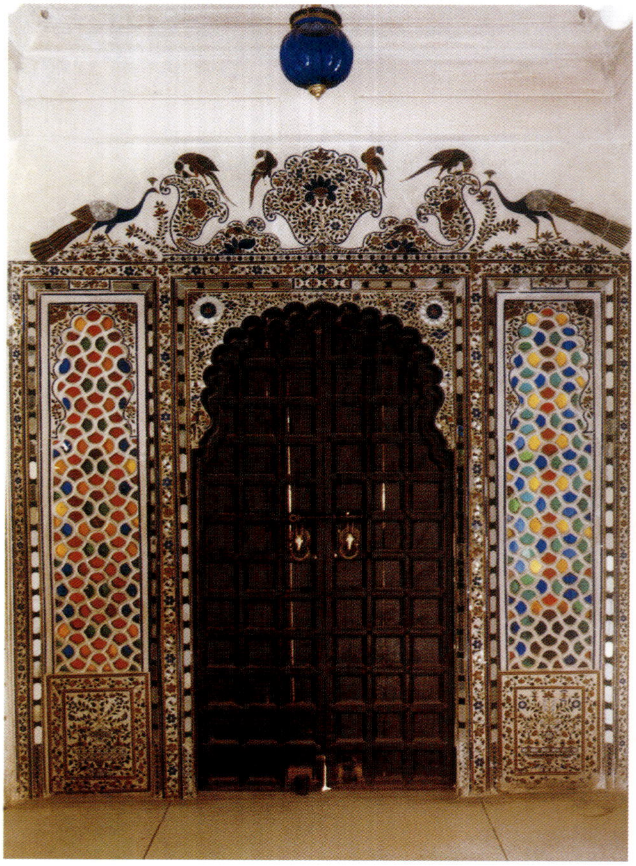

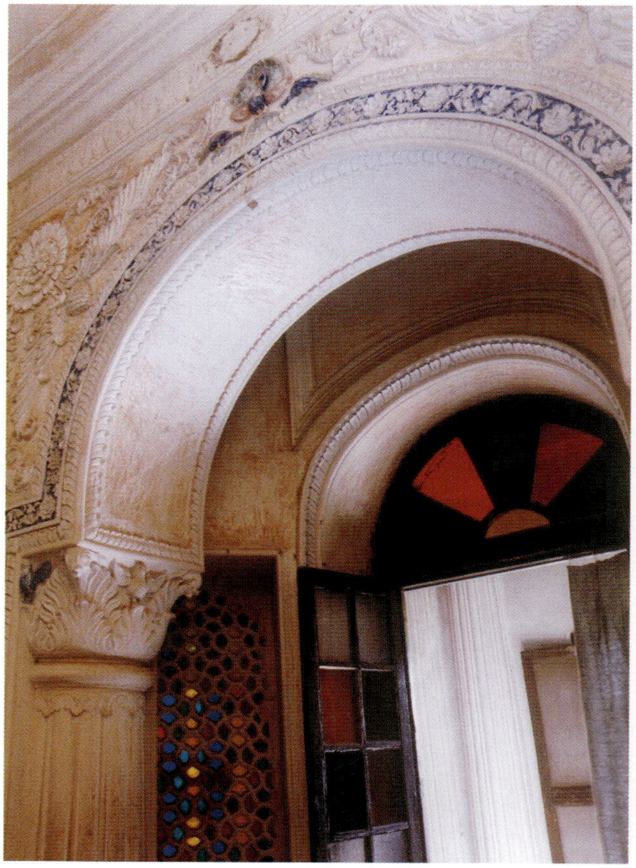

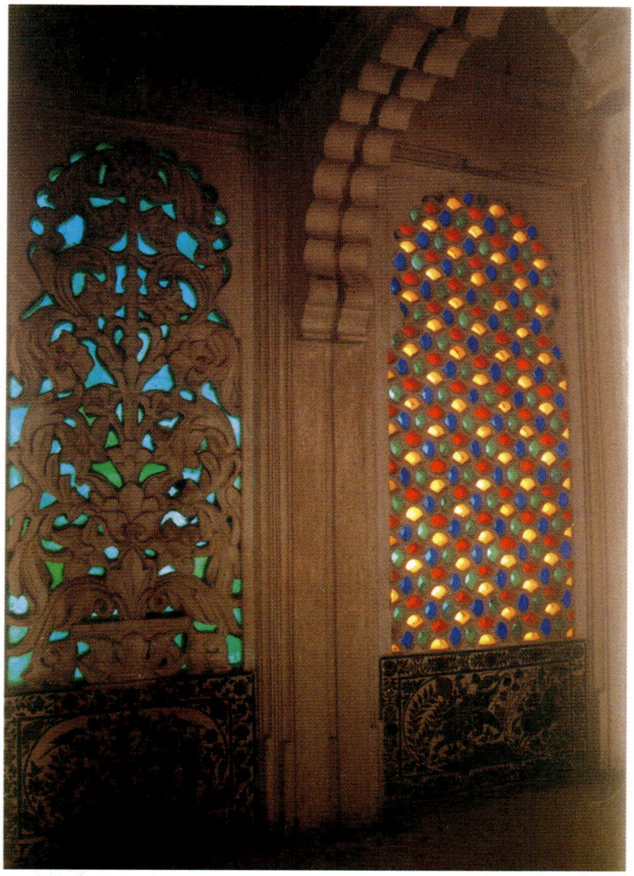

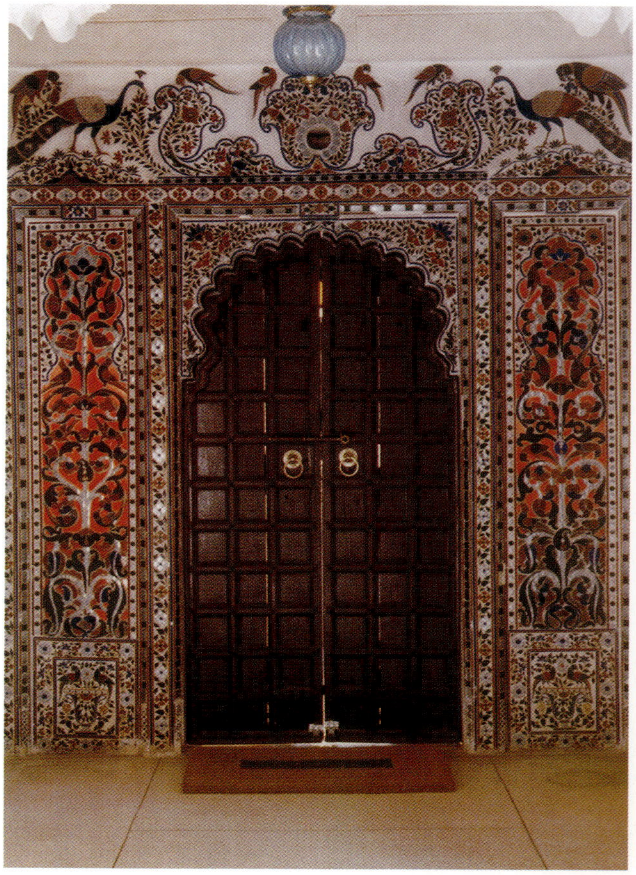

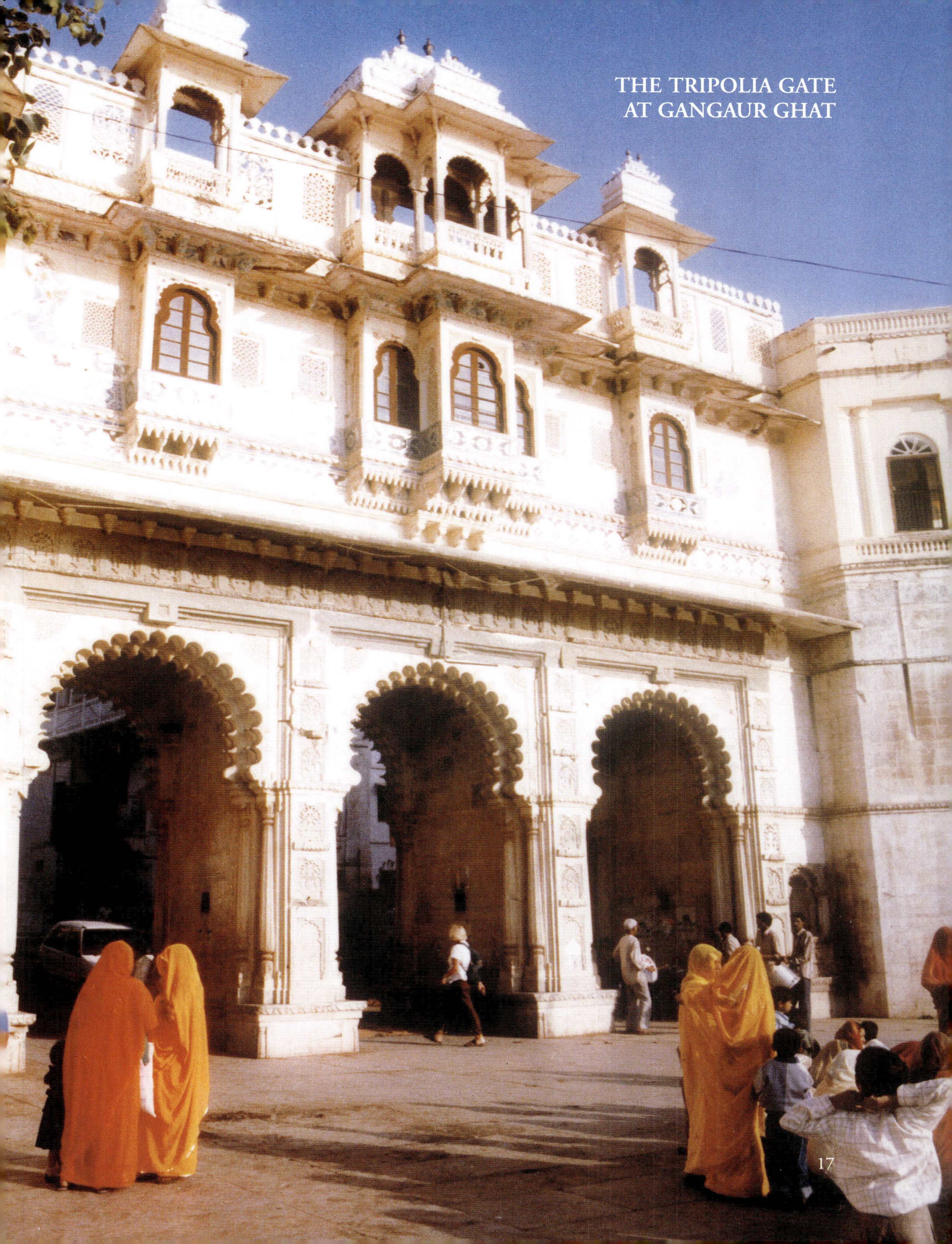

THE TRIPOLIA GATE AT GANGAUR GHAT

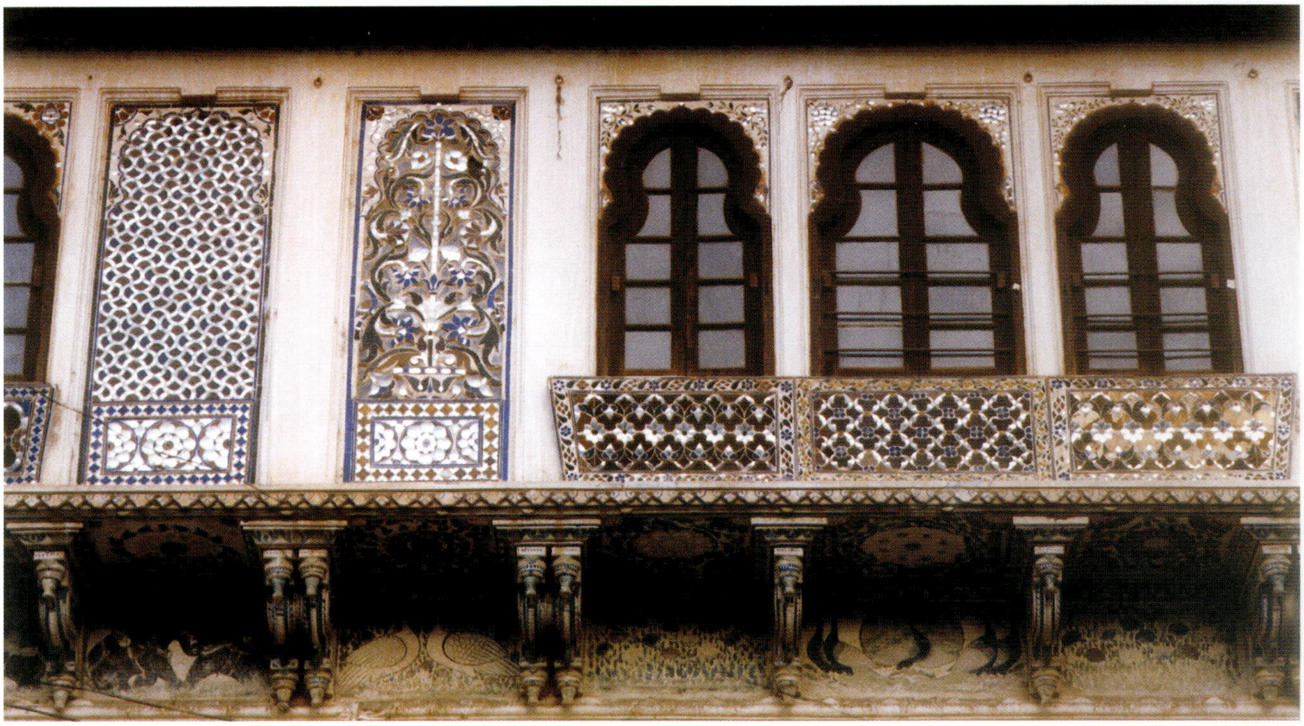

Mirror and glass mosaic worked into complex patterns form the exquisite detail above the Tripolia.

High above the Tripolia, amongst the domes and finials. The architectural feature crowning the gate is known as the Badi Burz.

KANCH MAHAL (GLASS PALACE)

The princes' living quarters were situated on the first floor above *Kuan Chowk*, the outermost courtyard. In arranging the accommodation this way, the inner courts of the *zenana* were protected, and also it ensured that no male visitors to the haveli, would pass close to the ladies quarters. The *diwan-e-khas* was the largest chamber in the *haveli,* but the WZCC offices now occupy the most spectacular rooms in the *mardana,* including the beautiful *Kanch Mahal* over the triple arched gate, the *Tripolia*.

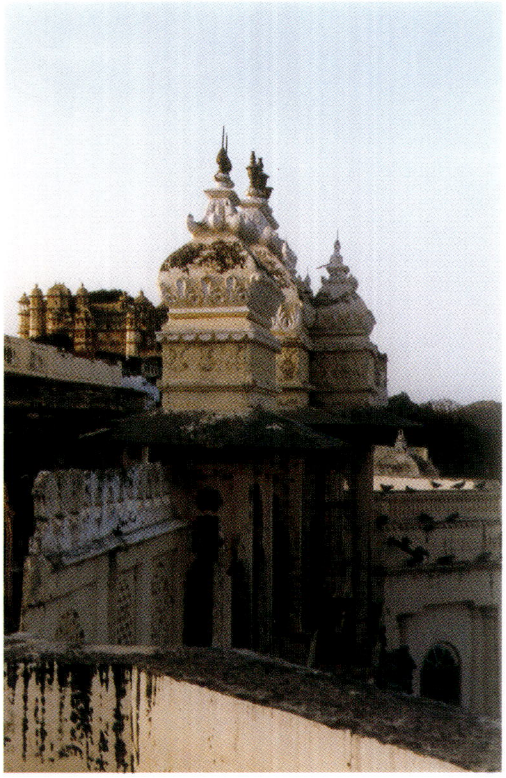

TRIPOLIA (TRIPLE ARCHED GATE)

This is probably the most famous feature of the *haveli* and indeed, one of the great landmarks of Udaipur, although it is in fact a comparatively recent addition. Maharaj Shakti Singh was responsible for the construction of the *Tripolia* in 1878, and the beautiful *Kanch Mahal* (Glass Palace) above it.

DURRIE KHANA

This chamber was originally carpeted with *durries* and served as a reception room *(baithak).* On occasions when public announcements had to be made, the populace would have been addressed from this room, which overlooks on one side, the Gangaur Ghat and on the other, the entrance court of the *haveli*. The office of the Director, WZCC now occupies the *durrie khana.*

THE WEST ZONE CULTURAL CENTRE

The West Zone Cultural Centre is one of seven zonal cultural centres, founded by the Government of India for the creative development of performing arts, visual arts, literary work, traditional folk and tribal arts. The areas covered by the WZCC are Rajasthan, Gujarat, Maharasthra, Goa, Dadra Nagar Haveli & Daman & Diu in the western region of India. There is an emphasis on the revival of vanishing arts and crafts forms and organising art & craft fairs and festivals.

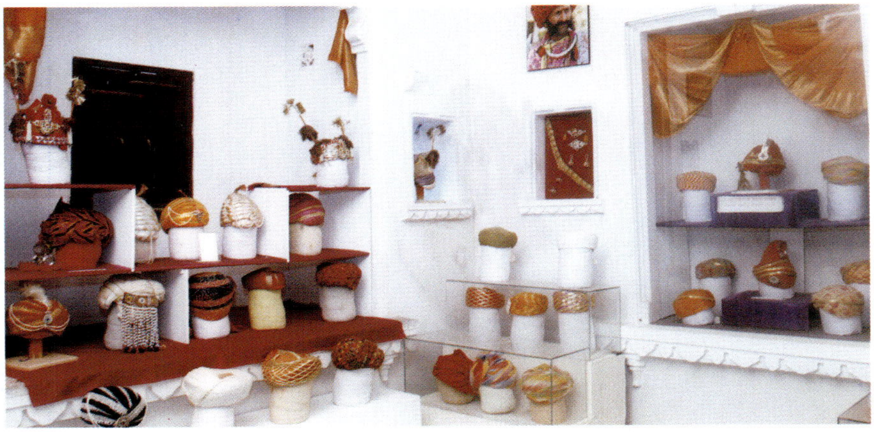

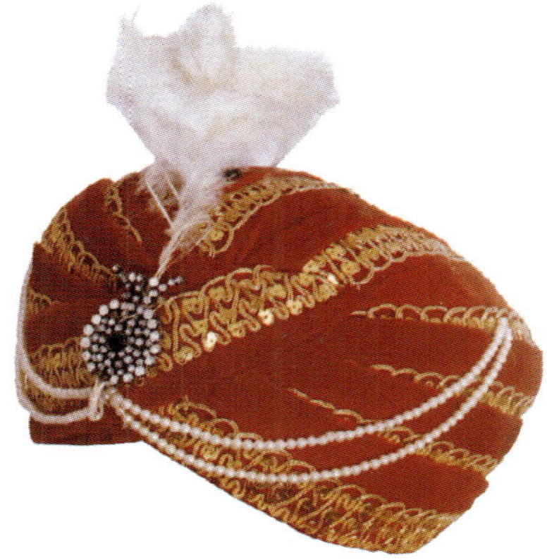

ART GALLERY & EXHIBITIONS

A number of exhibitions can be seen around the haveli: some are loosely related to the history of Mewar, such as the displays of turbans and Ladies' clothing and costumes.

The West Zone Cultural Centre, maintaining Bagore-ki-Haveli, has a responsibility to promote the art and culture of the regions under it's auspices.

The unique collection of models fashioned of thermocol (expanded polystyrene), tends to draw gasps of astonishment from visitors.

The Eiffel Tower, the Taj Mahal, the Leaning Tower of Pisa and the Victory Tower of Chittorgarh, as well as other brilliantly executed sculptures figure in the collection. The basement has been converted into an elegant art gallery, graced with traditional and contemporary fine art works. A thermocol model of Bagore Ki Haveli is the latest addition.

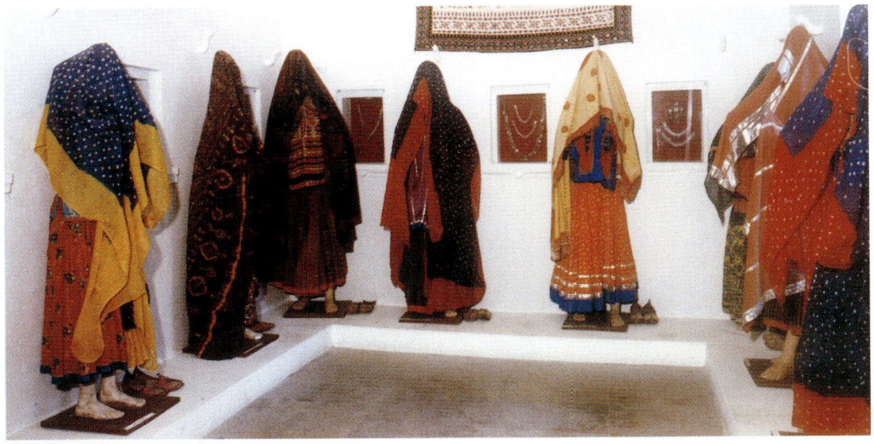

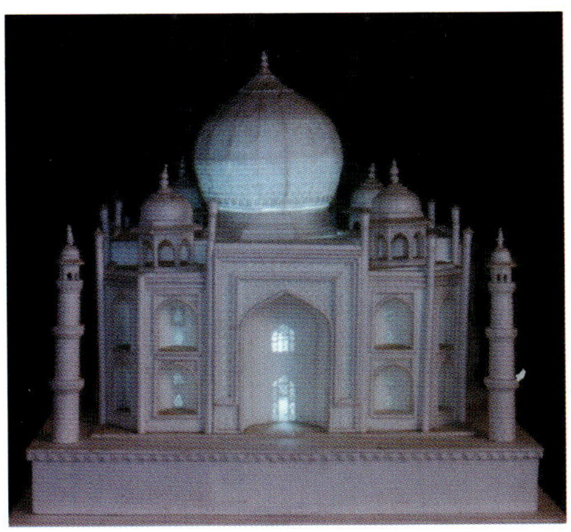

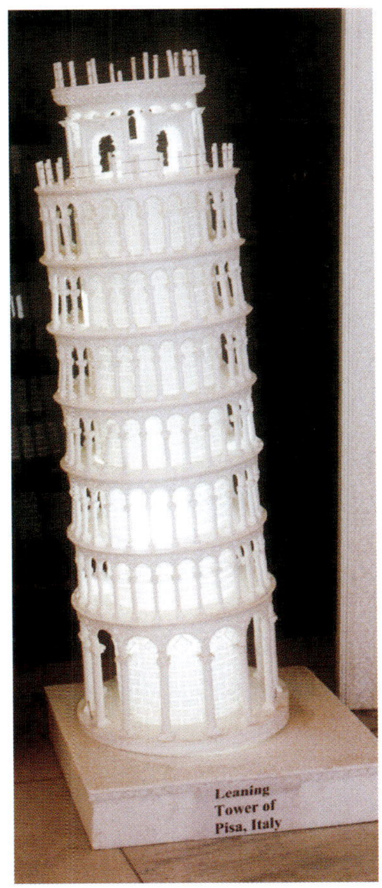

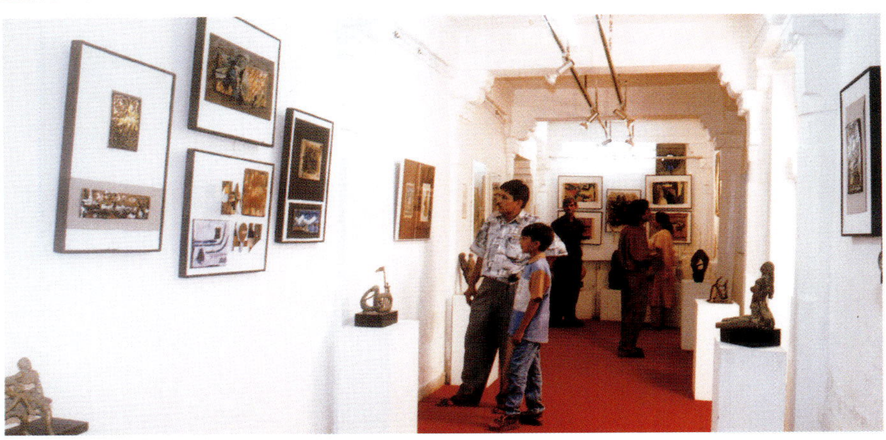

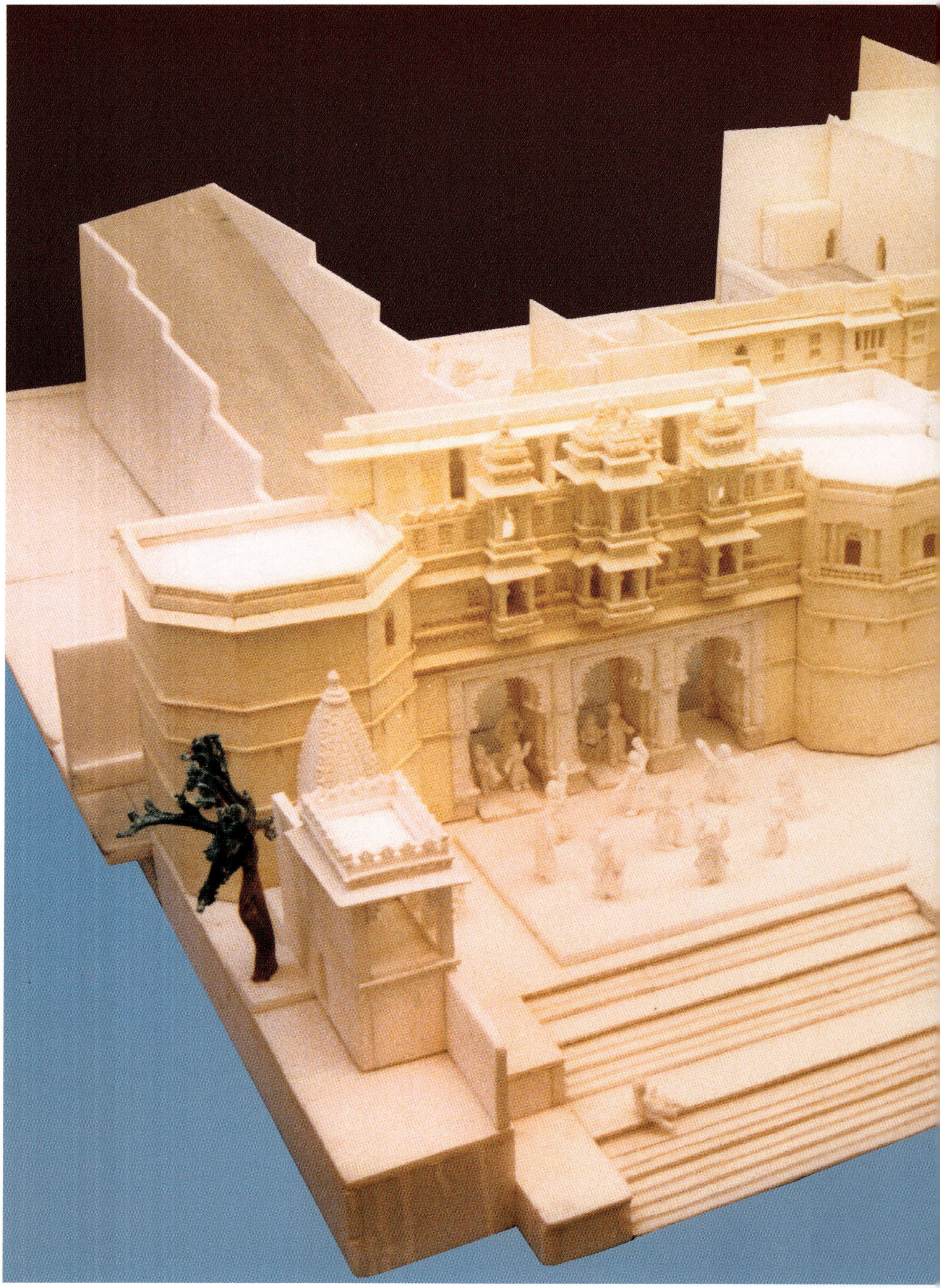

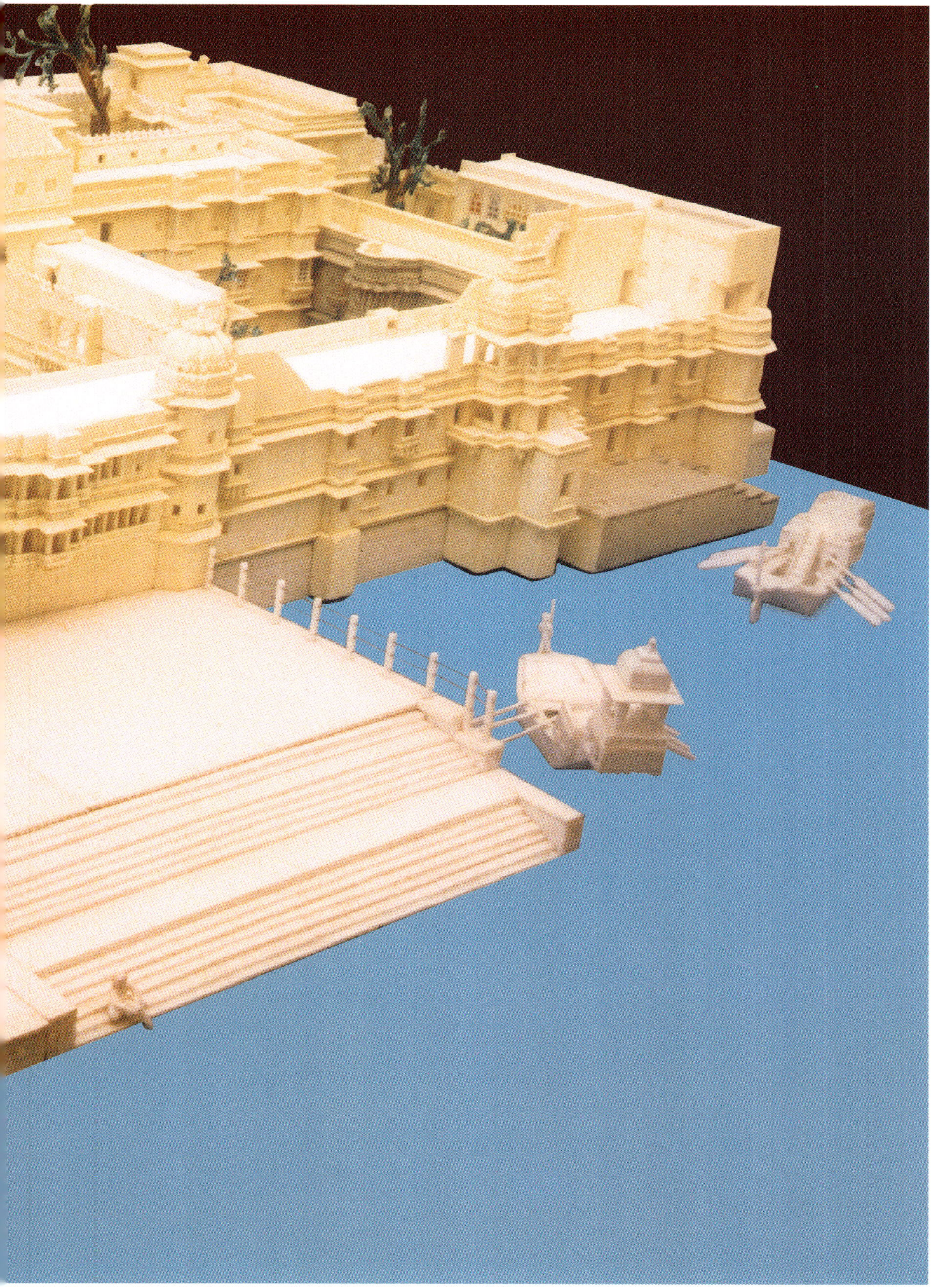

A Model of Bagore-Ki-Haveli made in Thermocol (Polystyrene)

MADHURĀṢṬAKAM

CHARMING KRISHNA - LORD OF SWEETNESS

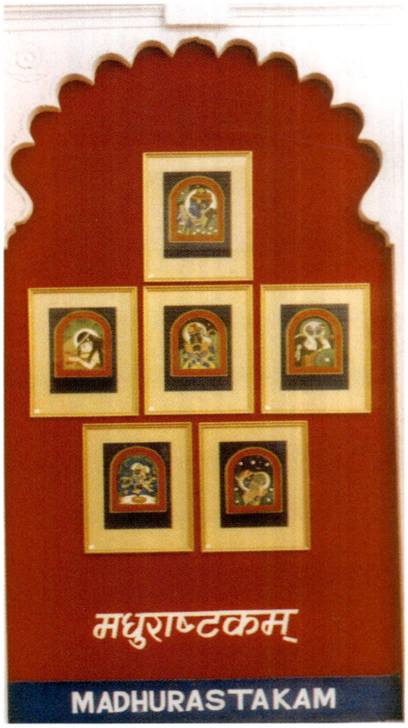

(above) the collection of Madhurastakam paintings displayed at the gallery room.

On the eleventh day of a bright 'Shravan' month in Gokul, Lord Krishna - God Himself appeared before Acharya Sri Vallabha. Vallabhacharya was so overwhelmed by the incomparable charming beauty of his beloved Lord and the highest sensation of divine pleasure that he composed Madhurashtakam (eight verses on divine sweetness).

In his song, Vallabhacharya described the extreme beauty and loveliness of Sri Krishna for the sake of those godly souls who had been forgetful of their original relationship with Lord. His sweet words are a continual flow of loving sentiments that sprang from his heart, from the divine vision of Sri Krishna's beauty. Devotees who cultivate divine emotions toward Lord Krishna with the feeling that he is their beloved can achieve complete satisfaction through the sweet waves of this spiritual love experience.

The word 'madhura' expresses the emotional attraction for loving union by the contemplation of the irresistibly radiant beauty of Sri Krishna's divine form. The form of Lord Krishna holds in itself the totality of divine pleasure, supreme bliss and loving sentiments, which has been proved by many saints and seers.

The Shrutis (holy scriptures) state that soul becomes extremely joyful when comes in contact with the charming beauty and loveliness of Lord Krishna. The presence of Sri Krishna's divine form and everything connected with him - His intimate associates; His games; His pets; His flowers .... bring bliss and extreme charm to those experiencing it. All of His surroundings with these lovely songs of Sri Vallabhacharya pour a constant flow of charming sweetness into the full bloomed heart of his followers.

(below) view of the permanent exhibition.

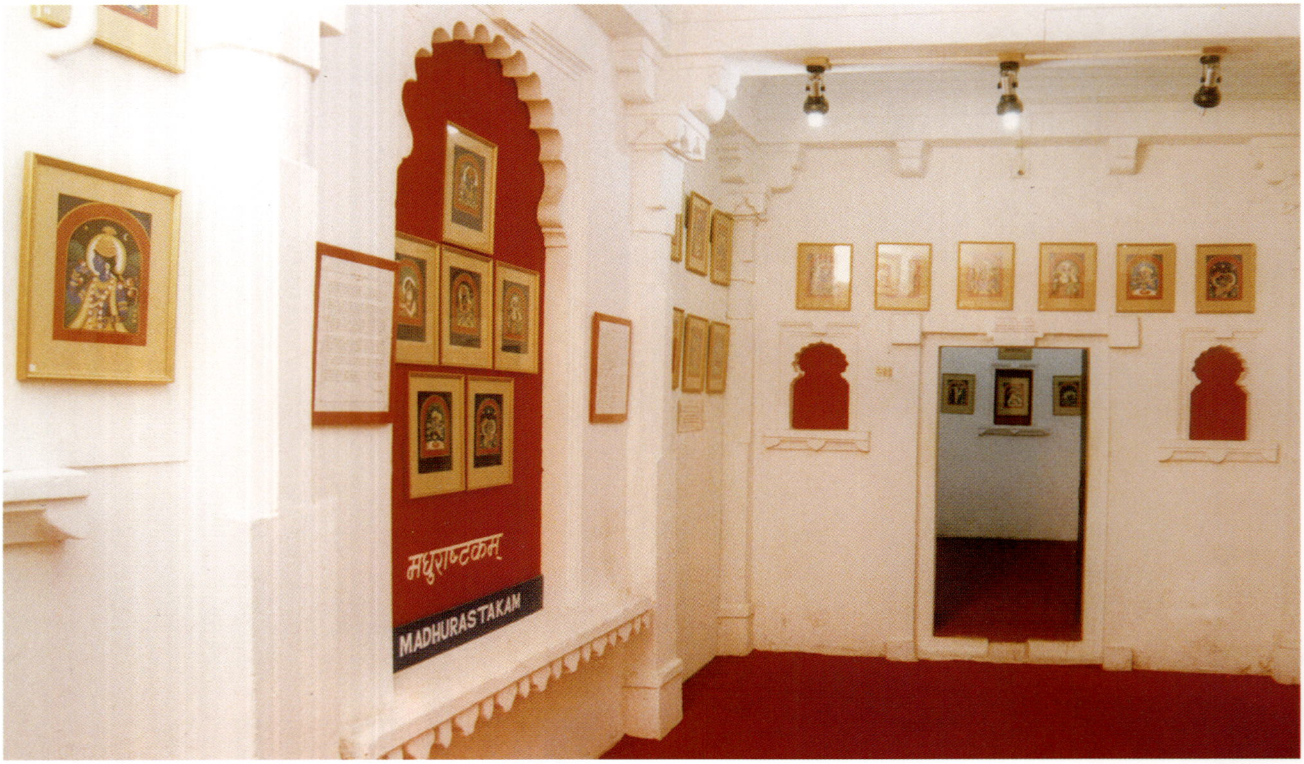

MADHURADIPATER AKHILAM MADHURAM

Lord of charming sweetness, entirely sweet ......

This loving flow of his charming beauty washes away from the heart all misfortunes and purifies the soul, making it acceptable for entrance to the sacred games. Prosperity, strength, fame, beauty, knowledge and renunciation are the six divine powers eternally present in the almighty Godhead, Lord Krishna. The power of divine beauty called Sri holds the extremely attractive charm and loveliness of Lord Krishna. The divine nourishment of the soul by the incomparable charming beauty and extreme loveliness of Lord Krishna is called Pusti (grace) by Acharya Sri Vallabha.

Acharya Shri Vallabha established Pusti Marga, the path of nourishment of the soul solely with the help of divine grace. According to Acharyaji's teaching, Sri the divine power of beauty, charm and loveliness is the essence of seva (service) and worship.

The divine form of Lord Krishna worshipped in Pusti Marga is called Srinatha the lord of charming beauty. An everlasting flow of grace spring out of the ocean of charming beauty and splendor of Sri Nathji and his various games.

Hungarin artist Rozalia Hummel – Radhika Priya born in 1946 came to India in the year 1981. She studied with the living masters, Mr. Reva Shanker Sharma and Mr. Ghanshyam Sharma in Nathdwara and trained her skills in symbolism of sacred art. All those who appreciate divine, loving sentiments are invited to take a deep bath in this ocean of charming beauty and love, which can be seen in the form of 48 paintings of "Madhurashtakam" in a permanent exhibition at Bagore-ki-Haveli Museum.

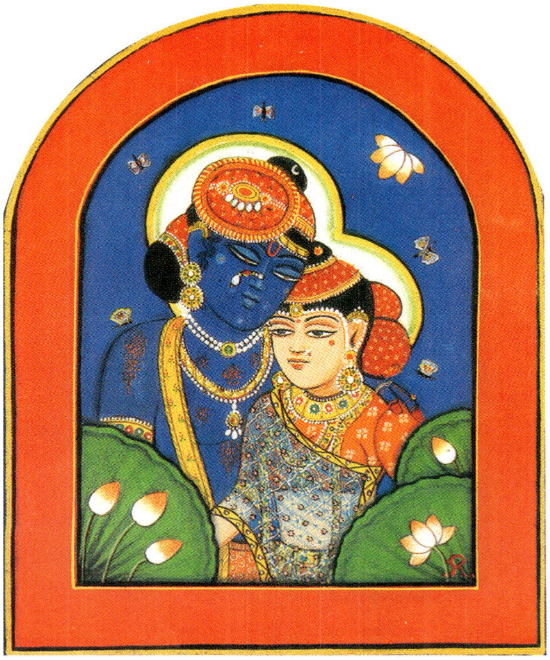

GAMANAM MADHURAM

After the embrace of the divine lovers, Lord Krishna remembers His beloved and hold the lotus offered by her with shaking hands, agitated by sentiments of great love. He is going to meet her very soon.

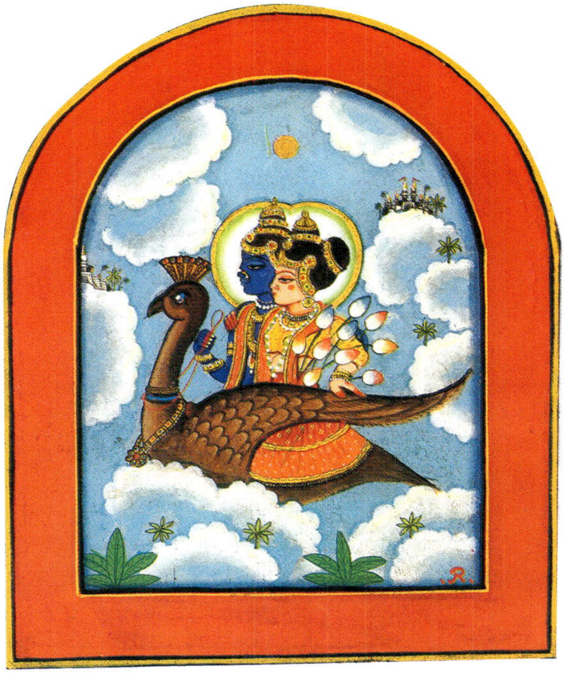

BHRAMITAM MADHURAM

Lord Krishna travels through the universe for the satisfaction of his devotees. One day, Satyabhama, his queen at Dwaraka, requested that He bring Her the parijata, the most beautiful flower from Indradeva's place. Lord Krishna left for Indralok to fulfill his queen's desire, flying graciously above the clouds.

'INDRA VIMAN'
THE ELEPHANT CHARIOT

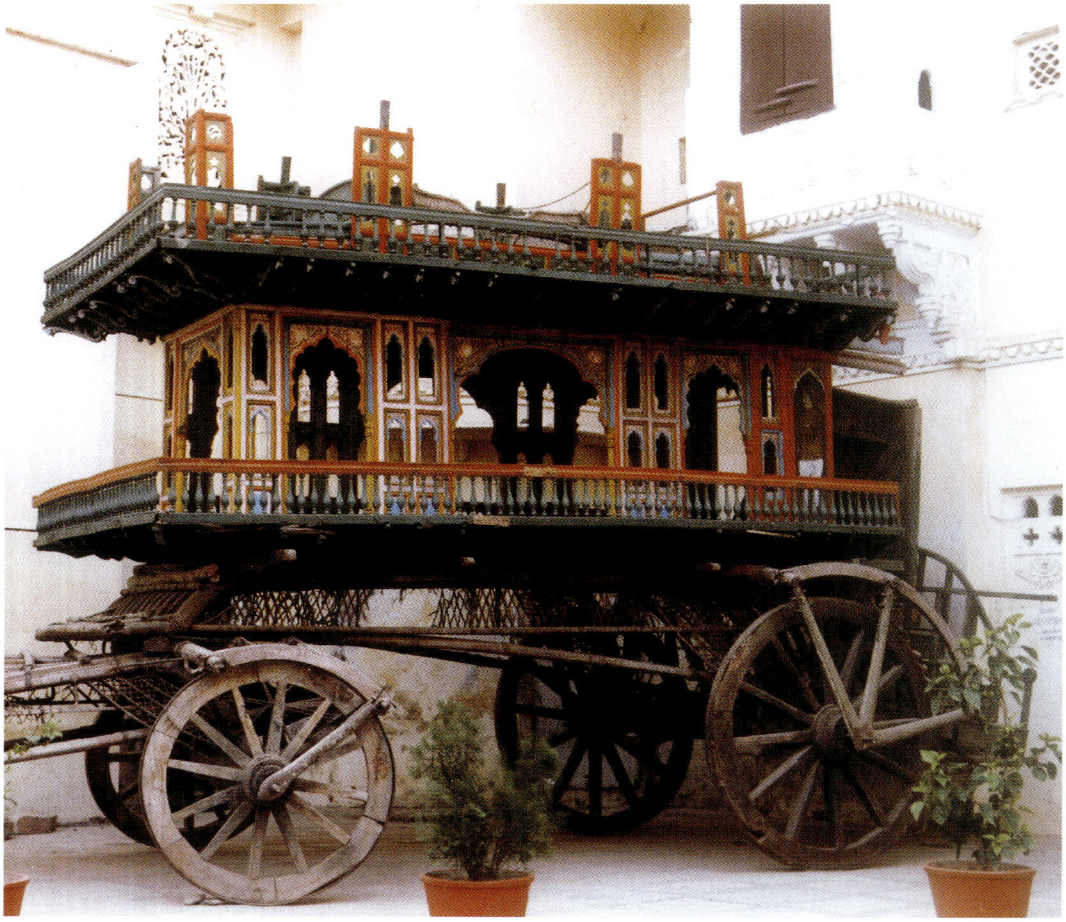

This chariot originally belonged to the King of Jhalawar, formerly a princely state in Eastern Rajasthan. The carriage was pulled by two elephants during various festivals such as Dusshera and Deepavali. The King of Jhalawar would take part in a procession from his seat on the carriage, where he could see, and be seen by, his people. After the merger of the state with the newly independent India, the carriage passed into the hands of the Government. The Jhalawar municipality gifted this chariot to the West Zone Cultural Centre for display.

The carriage was brought to Bagore-Ki-Haveli in a very dilapidated condition. It was carefully restored by the West Zone Cultural Centre, Udaipur. 'Indra Viman' is currently on display in the open courtyard leading to the entrance of Bagore-Ki-Haveli.